SHARING GOD'S GRACE

50 Years of Missionary Service in Brazil

GENEVA POOLE

randall house
114 Bush Rd | Nashville, TN 37217 | randallhouse.com

Sharing God's Grace
© 2010 by Geneva Poole

Published by Randall House Publications
114 Bush Road
Nashville, TN 37217
Visit www.randallhouse.com for more information.

All rights reserved. No part of this publication may be reproduced, stored in a retrieval system, or transmitted in any form or by any means—electronic, mechanical, photocopy, recording, or any other means—except for brief quotation in critical reviews, without the prior permission of the publisher.

All Scripture quotations are taken from The Holy Bible, King James Version.

ISBN-13: 9780892656059

Printed in the United States of America

Called by God's grace to reveal His Son.
Gal. 1:15-16
Geneva Poole

⚜

Lovingly dedicated to our sons, Robert and John, who have the same love we have for sharing the Good News of salvation with others.

I humbly express my gratitude to the many people who encouraged me to put down on paper the stories Bobby and I shared with them. My special thanks to my husband, who verified the facts, read and reread the manuscript, and gave suggestions valuable to produce the finished work.

⚜

Called by Lodi grove
to cancel for 1.15.16
Lynne Doole

TABLE OF CONTENTS

	Preface ix
Chapter 1	The Beginning..1
Chapter 2	Getting to The Mission Field......................17
Chapter 3	Settling In 27
Chapter 4	Learning the Language and Customs 33
Chapter 5	Into the Work 53
Chapter 6	Testimonies Through The Years 81
Chapter 7	A Dark Land 125
Chapter 8	Family 133
Chapter 9	A Decade of Experiences 159
	Conclusion 177

PREFACE

My love for God started at a very young age. If I have my facts straight, I was born on a Sunday and the following Sunday I was in church. God was such an intricate part of my life that, even when sick, I would cry because I could not go to church. It was a joy to learn about God through the teaching of His Word.

Then one day I recognized that my love for God was so small, so stunted, so shabby, so stained with failure in comparison to His unconditional love for me. It was then I turned my heart and life over to the Lord. I have failed Him many times in my walk with Him, but He has never failed me.

It is my desire that this book will show forth the grace of Christ in Bobby's life as well as in mine. I want you to see God's grace at work, using Bobby and me, two servants God called for the purpose of showing forth His love to the people of a country not our own. The Scripture verse used on our first prayer card, which speaks clearly of this desire, was, "God... called me by his grace, to reveal his Son in me that I might preach him among the heathen." (Galatians 1:15–16)

Word pictures are difficult to paint. It is no easy task to put the greatness of God into words. A phrase from Ephesians 1:6, "to . . . the glory of his grace," has come to my mind many times lately. May you visualize the glory of God's grace at work in and through our lives as you read this account of how God prepared us, united us, called us, sent us forth, and used us as His instruments. I trust that I have painted a picture of how God's grace flowed through us to the people we work among, and how that same grace flowed through those won to Christ into the lives of others, as churches came into existence in Ribeirão Preto, São Paulo, Brazil.

Geneva Poole

01.
THE BEGINNING

"Though thy beginning was small, yet thy latter end should greatly increase." JOB 8:7

What a Thanksgiving Day it was! This one took place during the years of the great depression, at which time many people in middle Tennessee used this holiday as hog-killing day. For the Poole family, in the year of 1935, things were different. Those who lived in Shady Grove Community rejoiced with the Poole family as the news spread from house to house that another child had been born.

It was indeed with thankful hearts that Blondell and Vernon Poole looked upon their newborn, a bouncing baby boy to whom they gave the name Bobby Luther, the name of Blondell's father Luther Albright. Blondell loved all eight of her children, each child with a special love. That love never lessened as the other seven children came along, making a total of fifteen, thus making Bobby the "middle" child.

Almost two years later, down in the farming community of Coward, South Carolina, I lay in my mother's arms, engulfed in the love of both parents. There were no grandmothers to cuddle me, since both had passed away before my birth.

Sometimes it is difficult to choose the right name for a newborn. Of course, Mary's sisters gave their opinions about a name. One of my aunt's suggested, "Since you gave your first child his father's name, John Dudley, why don't you give her our parents' names."

My dad quickly replied, "William. That is no name for a girl. Which of your mother's names should we use, Geneva or Caroline?"

My mother replied, "Instead of using Willie, the name Dad used, I prefer Billie. Why don't we give her the name Billie Geneva?" Thus, my name was chosen.

Both Bobby and I had many things in common: each of us had parents who loved and cared for us. We had Christian parents who loved and served the Lord; we both were brought up attending a Free Will Baptist church, and we were reared in a rural setting, giving us an appreciation for the outdoors. Having been born during the great depression gave us a conservative but positive outlook on life. Could it be that God was preparing us for each other? How could that be possible?

Bobby and I were fortunate enough to be raised in Christian homes. We will never forget the Christian heritage our parents, Sunday school teachers, and church family gave us.

One thing never questioned by both our families was whether or not we would go to church. Going to church filled the spiritual and social aspects of our lives when we were children.

I can vividly recall the revivals held at my home church each spring and fall. Most of the time, in those days, the church "was packed out" each night, so the children sat on the floor next to the pulpit to make room for more adults. Those evangelists preached down fire and brimstone. Even as a child, I had great joy when someone trusted Christ as Savior.

Daddy and Mama just did not know what was wrong. I, at age eight, could not walk because of crucial pain in my legs. Each time I ventured to walk tears streamed down my face and I cried out, "I can't!"—words I rarely used. I had a burning fever as well, that no medicine seemed to break. Without hesitation, my dad and mom took me to the family doctor who gave the prognosis—polio—and immediately put me in the hospital.

Dad hugged me as he left the hospital. It was so devastating to see his daughter suffering. He had to go off by himself to have a talk with God and a good cry, then afterwards home to be with his other three children.

My mom was different. She could not stand to leave me in my hour of suffering. Mom sat by my bed as the long hours slowly crept on, as if the fingers of death crouched nearby, always checking to see if my temperature had dropped any. Nurses came and went without seeing any visible sign of change in my little body.

Mom had been silently praying. Then, in the wee hours of the morning, she could not restrain herself any longer. She quickly knelt down beside the hospital bed and poured her heart out to the God she loved and served. Between sobs she prayed, "Gracious heavenly Father, I do not understand all of this, but You do. With all my heart, I want Your will to be done. I know You can heal. I give my child to You. If You can use her for Your glory and show Your grace through healing her, please do. I believe You will do what is best. In Jesus name, Amen."

Still kneeling and waiting before God, Mom had an inner peace to come over her. She arose and sat in the easy chair where she soon drifted off to sleep.

Upon awakening, she jumped up to check on me. "Thank you Lord. Thank you Lord!" came from Mothers' lips as she realized the fever was gone.

A miracle had happened. The next morning I was discharged from the hospital. My dad gently carried me to the car, but the entire time I was saying, "Let me down, daddy. I can walk. You don't need to carry me."

§§

A large family can be a lot of fun. Fun is not all that is necessary with so many mouths to feed, so many clothes to buy and to care for with so many attending school. During the Second World War times were difficult for practically everyone. It was getting more difficult for Bobby's family that already had ten children. Construction work was hardly going on. Daddy Poole was a plasterer and worked with decorative molding in fancy homes.

Bobby's family, like many other families, moved to Detroit to work in the factories. The five years in Detroit are indelibly stamped in Bobby's memory. He tells about some of the things that he and his brother, Carroll, did there—not only running errands for the factory workers near his house and becoming a part of a street gang, but also going to a Salvation Army Sunday school. He has often said, "I do not know what I would be today if we had stayed in Detroit." He expresses his gratitude that after five years the family moved back to the old log home place in Tennessee.

Back in Tennessee, at the age of twelve, Bobby accepted Jesus as his personal Savior. Naturally, that started things in another direction. Even though he was busy with farm work and school activities which included baseball, he was actively involved in his home church.

※

She is only a child. She does not understand what it means to be saved, was the attitude expressed by most of the adults when I was a child. Those words bothered me since I felt God dealing with me about salvation. Mothers are sometimes keen to the feelings and/or else led by God to do and say the right things at the right time. Deep conviction was already upon me. One afternoon while I was helping Mom shell beans the conversation led to the time I had been in the hospital with polio.

"I do not understand just what happened there in the hospital," I commented to my mother.

"I do. It was nothing short of a miracle of God," Mom replied. "Your daddy and I were both crushed with the diagnosis. I remember during the night crying, praying and turning you over to the Lord to use you in any way he saw fit. I believe God spared you for some special purpose."

Some special purpose! Those words went over and over in my mind. I could not get away from them; there was one problem. I kept thinking, *How could God use me if I have never accepted Christ as Savior?*

The time had come; I could wait no longer. At the age of thirteen hot tears streamed down my face and joy filled my heart when on Mother's Day I gave my dear mother the very best present. I accepted Christ as my personal Savior and on Father's Day followed the Lord in baptism. I did not plan it that way, but that is just the way it happened.

※

Christmas was always a special time. Each year my home church held festivities with a special program, a very large Christmas tree and exchange of gifts. I was always in the midst of such festivities, taking part in all plays or programs. Memorization seemed to come easily; therefore, often I was chosen for a longer speaking part.

One particular Christmas the program included a three-act play. The first act took place on a cold street where I played the part of a street child, the second in the church where I was studying the Word and the third on the mission field where I was a missionary. I was pouring my heart into the teaching of a group of children who had met on that particular Christmas to hear the Christmas story, some for the first time.

After the program came the comments usually complimentary. One of them on that particular night came from the pastor, Bro. Arthur Williams, who lovingly put his arms around me, gave me a big squeeze and said, "Let God direct your life. You will make a good missionary."

I have never forgotten those words.

Then the very first missionaries came across my path, Harold and Josephine Stephens from South Africa. At our church service, they gave a very vivid description of their work, of the dangers and of the triumphs as well, putting special emphasis on the dear people who came to know the Lord as personal Savior through their ministry.

The big python snakeskin was very impressive. I was reared in the lowland of South Carolina where a snake or two could be seen making its way across the road quite often. I remember the rattlers of a rattlesnake that my dad brought home and how he explained that a section was added to the rattler each time the snake shed its skin. Then I thought, *I could never consider a place where there was a possibility of an encounter with one of those huge monsters. In fact, I hate snakes, both kinds of them, dead ones and live ones.*

During the invitation, I was restless because I was fighting an inward battle. Had not my mother told me that God had healed me for a special purpose? Was this His purpose?

While the invitation continued, I squirmed a little; I wanted to resist. Nevertheless, at the same time felt as if I must go forward to be willing to do whatever God wanted me to do and to go where He wanted me to go. I made my way to the front of the church. *I want to go where God wants me to go.* My thoughts continued, *Even if it is to Africa among the people where there are big snakes.*

※

The Poole family was faithful in attendance at Shady Grove FWB Church in middle Tennessee. Sometimes, when taking visitors or during revival, they loaded up all the children on the tractor wagon (almost like a good old hayride) and off to church they would go. Of course, the fun ride was short lived since the distance was only about a mile. Bobby allowed the Spirit of God to work in his life.

He never got away from his decision to accept Christ as Savior and serve Him even though sports were high on his priority list. His dream during his high school days at good old Clarksville High was to become a professional baseball player. He had made the team and played as pitcher. It made him feel so good to pitch especially during the winning games.

There were also other possibilities, which often passed through his mind: *It sure would be good to go to agricultural school since I will probably be a farmer.* His high school graduation came and went with still no definite plans. Summer was quickly passing. Then the answer to his future came just before the school year of 1954-55. With cowboy boots on his feet and his application in his hand, he headed off to Nashville on the opening day of school to see about the possibility of entering Free Will Baptist Bible College. He told himself that he would go for one year and then transfer to an agricultural college. After his first year, he decided to go back one more year, since he felt God speaking to him about the ministry. That move changed his future and led him to continue on the four years and then one more year at Columbia Bible College in South Carolina.

Of course, while at Free Will Baptist Bible College he was exposed to FWB missionaries as well as to a few others. Each time a missionary came to share about his particular place of service, that place weighed heavily on his heart for days.

Bobby knew nothing about the giant country of Brazil except the sparse, outdated information from a geography book, but even with so little information, he could not get away from the idea of going to Brazil as a missionary. There was one great problem: Free Will Baptists had no work in Brazil.

Unlike Bobby, I had made definite plans to attend Free Will Baptist Bible College almost since the night I accepted God's missionary call upon my life. During my high school years I let my friends know of my desire to be a missionary, and I made plans to attend our denomination's college. The "class prophecy" given at my high school graduation had me serving in South America fulfilling my dream to be a missionary.

It was not easy for my parents to give their consent for me to go all the way from near Florence, South Carolina, to Nashville, Tennessee to attend college. Back in those days, the trip from Florence to Nashville took fifteen hours by car and twenty-three by bus over narrow mountain highways. There was no shortcut to Nashville. My family, especially my dad, tried to persuade me to go to Bob Jones University in our home state. It was near Clemson College where my brother was studying and Winthrop where my sister planned to attend.

College days hold fond memories for both Bobby and me. Three of our four years, we were in college together. We had a mutual respect for each other, and we were good friends.

Shortly after Bobby graduated in 1958, he became engaged to a young woman, who was also on her way to a mission field. It was a great disappointment to Bobby when the engagement was broken only a year later. But he rested in God's sovereignty to bring the right girl into his life at the right time.

That fall after his graduation, he enrolled in the master's program at Columbia Bible College. God also gave him a place of service as pastor of Little Star Free Will Baptist Church near Lake City, South Carolina. In this pastorate, he made a number of friends who have supported him as a missionary all these many, many years—in fact fifty of them.

That pastorate was like a bed of roses, with both the perfume and the thorns. He had won the confidence of the young people and led the church into full-time services. He thought the church was moving forward too fast for a country church at that time. He noticed that some people, who had never even heard him preach, came to the annual business meeting. Unaware of any problem, he went out into the church yard for the people to cast their vote of confidence, which was their annual custom. To his surprise, he did not receive the vote to stay as pastor. How heartbreaking! How devastating to a young minister! However, God saw to it that he did not have to dwell on the subject for long. Within two weeks, he was called to pastor High Hill Free Will Baptist Church, just a few miles away, where he stayed until he resigned to go to the mission field.

My last year at Free Will Baptist Bible College was a very trying time. My sister Mary Lou was beginning her second year at Winthrop College. Toward the end of September 1958, the campus doctor sent her home to get medical testing done. She stayed so tired and worn out all the time. Mary Lou never went back to college. The diagnosis was a rare blood disease—hemolytic anemia. Her red blood count stayed very low because the red blood cells were dying within thirty days when they should live approximately ninety days. She was in the hospital on a regular basis receiving blood in order to just stay alive.

Because of Mary Lou's condition weighing heavily on my younger sister, Betsy was having one asthma crisis after the other. Mom did not know whether to stay at home with Betsy or go to the hospital with Mary Lou, so she called me to come home for a while. I received permission to be away from my classes for as long as three weeks, so off to South Carolina I went.

My dad also had a surgery during that time. It almost seemed that our world was falling apart. After things calmed down a little, I took the twenty-three hour bus trip back to Nashville to finish my last semester of college.

Graduation was special in a number of ways. My family made the long trip to attend my graduation. Mary Lou was also able to make the trip. After graduation, I became engaged to a young man from my graduating class who also desired to go to a mission field. Things seemed to be taking a positive turn.

Once home, I was anxious about getting on with my life. Nevertheless, Dad asked me to stay with Mary Lou who was still in and out of the hospital and required more and more nursing care. That summer she developed abscesses that were very painful and required hot soaks, even at intervals during the night. With these developments, I became Mary Lou's nurse staying with her almost constantly both day and night. At the hospital and at home as well, I prayed with her, cared for her, joked with her, and played games with her when she felt up to it, just to pass the time.

The dreaded hour came on October 20, 1959. All of our family had gone down to Charleston to be there since Mary Lou was so critically ill. I was in the room with her and found that Mary Lou's watch had come off her arm. I picked it up and tried to put it back on her arm. Gasping for breath, she said, "No, you keep it until I get better." (Incidentally, thieves later broke into our house and lifted that watch during our first term of service in Brazil.) A few hours later, she left that frail body and was ushered into the presence of our Lord. Mom and I were at her bedside watching her. She looked as if she had gone to sleep—she simply stopped breathing.

Mom ran out of the room to announce her death to the other members of the family who were in a small sitting room. She said, "Mary Lou has gone to be with Jesus! She has left us and has gone to be with Jesus!"

Many of the nurses and doctors, who had become real friends during the thirteen hospital stays, came by to give the family a word of condolence.

One doctor even offered to drive our family the 110-mile trek home.

As friends and family gathered around the Hicks family, I became more aware of God's blessings upon us. Those days linger in my memory. During all the months of taking care of my sister, my fiancé had only participated by letter. I needed him, but he was never present.

§§

Mary Lou's death led into another phase of my life. Bobby Poole, a college friend, was living in Lake City, South Carolina. He read the notice in the obituary column of my sister's death while he himself was very sick with a kidney infection. He decided that he must get in touch with me to show his respect, so he got out of his sickbed and came to our country home where Mary Lou's body lay in wake.

I had been longing for an opportunity to have someone to talk to who would pray with me; but during the time we were talking Bobby almost fainted because of his physical condition.

Bobby talked to me about my fiancé and did not understand why he was not with me at a time like that. Bobby even offered to go to Columbia, South Carolina, to bring him to me. I refused to allow such a thing.

I began thinking about my decision to be married to someone who seemed to have so little concern about me, but our correspondence continued. Some time later, he wrote me that he no longer desired to go to a mission field. That was the last straw. I knew I had to break the engagement and return his ring.

§§

One afternoon of the week following Mary Lou's funeral, I was in my room trying to put some order to my thoughts about what to do next. A school superintendent from the St. Stevens school district, who had been a former neighbor and my eighth-grade history teacher, came searching for me. The sixth-grade teacher at Cross Elementary School had to leave because of her husband's job transfer. The vacancy was mine if I accepted the position.

I gave all the arguments I knew: "I have no training in elementary education or in teaching." "I only went to Bible College." "I do not have a teacher's certificate." "I have not taken the national teachers' exam!" He gave me assurance that the job was mine, because even if he could not get me a provisional certificate, there were provisions of county funds to secure my salary.

By the following Monday I had found a place to live and was in the classroom. God supplied that place to keep me useful and busy, helping me not to dwell on the heavenly homegoing of my sister who was almost like a twin to me. Until I moved to Nashville to attend college the two of us were inseparable.

God used those months at Cross Elementary School to set the direction for my life. Since that first experience with the classroom, I have spent much time in one, both in the U.S. and Brazil.

Naturally, I was home for the Christmas holidays. Bobby did not go to Tennessee since he was the pastor of a church in South Carolina. He thought about me, even though we had not seen one another since the funeral in October. On his way to Florence, he decided to drop in to see me. What a disappointment came his way, since the visit had to be brief. He found me in bed, sick with the flu and burning up with fever.

Our paths did not cross anymore until springtime when we both went to Nashville for the Bible Conference. We traveled in two separate cars, but at the conference we sat together on several occasions. It was then that he began to notice me, but there was one big obstacle: my engagement ring.

Shortly after the conference, we were together once again. The YPA (Young Peoples Auxiliary), with the cooperation of the women of the church, planned a banquet called "April Love." The banquet took place on the Saturday night before Easter Sunday.

One suggestion made was to invite Bobby Poole to bring a devotional on the love God showed in giving His Son. Since I knew him better than anyone else in our group, they asked me to extend the invitation to him.

I had already written to my fiancé inviting him to the banquet. He quickly replied that it would be impossible for him to be there. Actually, I was kind enough to ask permission to invite his friend Bobby Poole to escort me to the banquet. He agreed; so with that settled, I not only asked Bobby to speak, but also to be my escort.

I was very conscientious and did not feel exactly right about going with Bobby to the banquet. My schedule was a tight one. I was decorating the banquet hall later than I should have been, so I called Bobby and asked him to meet me there. He was so kind and understanding and presented me with the most beautiful orchid when he arrived.

The banquet was a success, the program was entertaining, and the meditation was great, not to speak of the scrumptious meal. How could I refuse to allow Bobby to take me home after and evening like that? So off we went!

On the way to my house, we talked about the state young people's banquet. Bobby asked me to allow him to escort me to that banquet also. I could not give him an answer that night, but politely said, "I have to go since I am on program; but I really don't know if, under the circumstances, I should go with you. I will think about it and let you know in plenty of time."

The invitation caused me to break my engagement and return the ring. What a relief I felt! I knew I was doing God's will. That freed me to accept Bobby's invitation as well, and I did.

Bobby picked me up in plenty of time to leisurely travel the forty miles. He immediately noticed that the engagement ring was no longer on my finger. His heart leaped with joy! That evening we had a lovely time together.

From then on, Bobby always found occasions to invite me to go with him. For instance, there was the week of services held to start a church, which became Grace Free Will Baptist Church in Lake City, South Carolina. Of course, I would have been there anyway, but he invited me to go with him. Then the speaker of the week needed someone to take him the one hundred and ten miles to Charleston to fly back to Oklahoma. Bobby took him and invited me to go along. Most of the day we spent enjoying the each others' company and sightseeing in Charleston.

Our spirits were bonding and, before long, Bobby and I began to take a more serious look at our situation. Bobby had already received his approval to go to Brazil as a single missionary and had plans to leave as soon as funds came in, which he hoped would be in September. He had already gone to Florida in the spring and was leaving his church on the first day of July to start full-time deputation. Things were shaping up for him to leave on time. There was one minor problem. He had already decided he wanted to marry me. However, I had not been approved by the mission board. That approval would be the sign of God's approval for me going to Brazil as Bobby's wife.

Bobby felt that perhaps there could be a problem of my parent's permission. When Bobby asked my parents for their permission to marry me, they readily agreed even though he would be taking me a very long way from home. In fact, Bobby was just the kind of man they wanted their daughter to marry. He became as a son to them. I never felt free to talk to my parents about any kind of disagreement that Bobby and I had, because I was certain that if they were to take sides they would take his.

That spring I received an unexpected letter from Rev. Robert Crawford, who at that time was the pastor of the Greenville Free Will Baptist Church in North Carolina. The letter extended an invitation for me to go to the church to meet the people, with the possibility of becoming the youth director.

During a weekend visit, I had a lovely time among the church family. One big problem I had to solve was my relationship with Bobby. While in Greenville, I had the opportunity of talking with Dr. Charles Thigpen about my future plans of becoming a youth director or going to the mission field.

It was a comfort to know that Dr. and Mrs. Thigpen would be praying with me. I felt at peace that God would lead.

In only a few days, the answer came from the church. They invited me to become their youth director. But God had also given me peace that I should not delay marrying Bobby and consequently going with him to the mission field. I was sure that God was opening the door. For many years, Mrs. Crawford teased Bobby about stealing their youth director.

§§

I got busy. First, I wrote asking for a missionary application form. I had previously sent in my preliminary application; therefore, with the first step completed, I had saved time. When the form arrived, I worked hard to get it sent back as quickly as possible. The form had to be in the office before the National Association meeting, which convened in California that year. Neither Bobby nor I could go. Even without meeting with the board, I received approval to go to Brazil. Foreign Missions director Rolla Smith told Bobby that the board gave their approval based on Bobby's good judgment.

Some months earlier I had accepted an invitation to teach in Youth Camp, and Bobby and I had received invitations to speak at the Women's Retreat in South Carolina as well. Both of these were scheduled in the month of August, so our wedding date was set for September 4, 1960.

Our going to the field was delayed until December of that year. Bobby did not mind one bit.

§§

It was a simple, but pretty wedding on a Sunday afternoon. I wore a traditional long white gown and my groom wore a navy blue suit. The ceremony took place at Tabernacle Free Will Baptist Church in Coward, S. C. on Labor Day weekend, September 4, 1960. My dad walked me into the church and down the aisle to the front, where he gave me to Bobby. Looking into Bobby's eyes and speaking from my heart, I recited the poem "How do I love Thee" by Elizabeth Barrette Browning.

When the time came for the vows, Bobby and I faced each other and said them to each other, after which Bro. Louis Holiday pronounced us husband and wife. It appeared that he was more nervous than either Bobby or I.

After a reception on the church lawn, we were off to North Carolina for a weeklong honeymoon.

It was cool in the Mountains of Maggie Valley. A dear Free Will Baptist couple, Bruce and Nellie Sealey, allowed us—as well as many other couples over the years—to use their cabin for our honeymoon. It was a one-room cabin with a nice size fireplace and a wood stove as well. Of course, Mr. Sealey had plenty of firewood in the bin.

Among the memorable things we tried was to swim in small water hole where the creek had been dammed up. Bobby jumped in, but I tested it first with my big toe. He came out almost as fast as he went in. The cold mountain water in September was not very pleasant for swimming. In fact, we stayed inside by the fire more than we stayed outside.

The time of our honeymoon was some years before Maggie Valley became a tourist attraction. We will never forget the beauty, quietness, and the oneness we felt with each other and in the presence of God.

The words of the old hymn, "O to Be Like Thee" by Thomas O. Chisholm, became Bobby's favorite song and prayer and has become my heartbeat as well. That song expressed Bobby's desire to be pure like his Redeemer. He has often expressed a longing for God to stamp His own image on his heart and fill him with compassion and love, as well.

02.
GETTING TO THE MISSION FIELD

"So they, being sent forth by the Holy Ghost, departed...." ACTS 13:4

During the week of our honeymoon, the Canton Free Will Baptist Church was holding revival services, but we were not aware of it until we went into Canton on Wednesday night for prayer meeting. The Sealeys extended us an invitation to return on Friday night and stay overnight in their home. Since Bobby and I were leaving on Saturday morning and Canton was a few miles nearer to our destination in South Carolina, we took them up on their offer. That honeymoon venture led to a lasting friendship with these precious servants of God.

At the church's next business meeting, the church was to decide about taking on new mission support. A brother got up and said, "Do you remember that couple who came twice to our revival services while on their honeymoon? I think any couple who will go to church on their honeymoon deserves our support." The church took on support for us, and it has continued down through the years.

With that quiet week fresh in our memories, we busied ourselves in preparing to get to the field. We spent the first two weeks in revival services at McColl Free Will Baptist Church and Tabernacle, my home church in Coward, South Carolina. They were refreshing weeks which resulted in friendships that have been enduring ones.

To raise our support and get to the field, we were on our own without a salary, which was the system in those days. Bobby received ten dollars per service and I received five dollars each time I spoke as much as 10 minutes. The first salary of 150 dollars only began the month we reached the field. When we put figures down on paper we had real doubts about the financial end of missions, but we never doubted our call to Brazil. That is what kept us going; and God supplied the rest!

About six weeks after our wedding and into deputation, we made our first trip to Tennessee. Needless to say, I was apprehensive and a bit nervous, with butterflies in my stomach, since I had not met any of Bobby's family. Such thoughts as, *Will they accept me? Will they approve of me? Will they be happy that Bobby is taking a helpmate with him to Brazil?*, ran through my mind.

Our first stop was at Earl and Edna Baggett's, the home of Bobby's sister who still lives in Nashville. They were a lovely family of five and I quickly bonded with them, giving me a feeling of being accepted and loved.

The next day we went on out into the country to be with Bobby's family. During the forty-mile trip, the apprehension took control of me again; however, upon arrival, it did not take many minutes to feel loved and to love. Mrs. Poole was an extraordinary woman who spent most of her time for her family of fourteen living children. One child, Della Ann, had died a month before her first birthday from double pneumonia, about six years before Bobby was born. I could see a love and closeness in the Poole family, and I was happy to be a part of it. The sisters-in-law's were so interwoven into the family that it was difficult to know who was a blood kin and who was an in-law.

Bobby's maternal grandmother, Granny Albright, was still alive but bedridden. Bobby took me to meet most of his uncles and aunts. He also kept talking about taking me to meet Granny Albright. He seemed to be elated about going to see Granny Albright. Since I had not known my own grandmothers, I was looking forward to having a grandmother.

We drove all the distance of about a mile out to Granny Albright's house. Bobby seemed so proud that we were going to Granny's. After Bobby introduced me to Granny, lying there in her bed, she looked me up one side and down the other— from head to foot and back again. Then in a voice, which sounded to me like disdain, she finally said, "Bobby, what did you get yourself into?" Since I had already found myself in the comfort zone of the family, there were no butterflies that time. Nevertheless, immediately after Granny's remark I was very uncomfortable and felt as if I were sitting on pins and needles. Bobby, along with her other grandchildren, was never close to Granny. He told me that he could not remember her ever giving him an affectionate squeeze or a word of love.

On the trip to Tennessee, we went back to Free Will Baptist Bible College for the missionary conference. The last night of the conference was the commissioning service for a number of missionaries. It was possibly the largest number of foreign missionaries ever commissioned by Free Will Baptists in one service. Among those commissioned were Dr. and Mrs. Miley, Bill and Glenda Fulcher, Bobby and Sue Aycock, and Bobby and me. We had met all the requirements except raising the rest of our funds and would soon be on our way to the field of Brazil.

Our travels took us to North Carolina, South Carolina, Virginia, Maryland, Georgia, Florida, Alabama, Tennessee, and Arkansas. In those good old days, we made all-night trips to get to the next place of service. Remember, there was no interstate system. The night after our commissioning service, we left Nashville, Tennessee, to go to a Women's Auxiliary Convention in the southern part of Georgia. Sometime in the early morning hours, our '52 Ford began to make a terrible knocking noise. Getting to a closed service station, Bobby decided we had better stop. At that hour of the morning nothing was open, so we decided the best thing to do was to get some rest. I took the backseat and Bobby the front, and off to sleep we went. As soon as daylight appeared, we both woke up. The first thing on our list was to try to find a phone. There was no pay phone available. When the station opened, Bobby tried to get in touch with the president of the auxiliary convention, but there was no answer. With no other way of communicating, we tried to find a taxi, but that did not work out (probably because of the cost to take us over a hundred miles). When we finally did get in touch with the president, she told us that they knew something had happened and the convention was sending one hundred dollars toward our account, which was an excellent offering, especially since we had not even been present. In those days, most of the offerings were less than fifty dollars, averaging around thirty-five dollars. The needed funds did come in, thus making it possible for us to arrive in Brazil on the date set, December 14, 1960. God did not fail then and has never failed since.

With only a couple of months until departure date, Bobby's brother Carroll supplied the need for another vehicle. He had already started his tile business, so he had a pickup and a car. He and Marybelle graciously agreed to lend us their '55 black Ford and insisted on us using the car. That offer was a God-sent one.

༄༅

We had applied for and received our passports. The next step was to get our visas. That meant getting a physical and numerous papers to take with us to Baltimore, Maryland, to apply for the permanent visa. My dad was kind enough to insist that Bobby use his '58 Chevrolet for the Baltimore trip.

That trip was an eventful one. We had driven all night to get to Baltimore by the time the consul's office opened. Not very far out of Baltimore, the alternator had problems. We stopped at a garage where the mechanic got started working on the car right away, making it possible for us to arrive in Baltimore during the morning office hours. To our surprise—and what a pleasant surprise it was!—Bobby and Sue Aycock were also at the consulate getting their visas to go to Brazil. We gave all of our paperwork to the consul, who checked things out and told us to return around 3:00 that afternoon for the visas. What a relief! Things had worked out for us to have our visas in hand that very day.

Ken Walker, Bobby's college classmate and former pastor, was along with the Aycocks and my sister Betsy was with us. We took advantage of the time and visited several places of interest in the Baltimore area.

We went back to the consulate at the appointed time to get our visas and headed out to Norfolk, Virginia to spend the night with my great aunt and uncle. Well, "headed out to" are not exactly the right words, for we headed out *from* since Betsy had the map turned upside down and directed Bobby to go out the north side of the city. We tried to make light of the situation, but Betsy did not. She decided to lie down in the backseat. Instead of going to sleep, she began to think about her sister going off to Brazil and leaving her family. She began to breathe harder and harder. I knew we were in for trouble. Betsy was having an asthma attack. By the time we arrived in Norfolk, Betsy had taken several doses of medicine with little relief, so off to the hospital we went. It was well past 1:00 a.m. when finally Betsy got relief. We spent a very short night at Uncle Sam and Aunt Helen's.

The next morning there was no time to delay because we had to be back in the Florence area for the Saturday night service at New Town Free Will Baptist Church. There was no rest for the weary, since the Sunday morning service was one hundred and ten miles away in Charleston and the night service in Savannah, Georgia, another one hundred miles away. All of the traveling was done on simple two-lane roads. In fact, I have never before felt the fatigue I felt during that service in Savannah. The next day we went to Jacksonville, Florida for a service that night and Tuesday on to Lakeland, Florida, for services in the area. Our two-week stay in Lakeland with Bobby's oldest brother Junior and his family was what we needed. We had a lovely and restful time there in Junior's home. During the day, the girls were at school and Junior and Wilkie were at work. That left Bobby and me to go and do as we desired. Practically every night we visited a church in the area.

❧❧

Those were the days before the provision closet of the Women's Auxiliary. Under the leadership of Maude Coffey, the women of South Carolina did a lot to get supplies for us. Before leaving for the field, she led the women in purchasing an excellent supply of Tupperware. I still have a few of those original pieces after fifty years. During our first year on the field, Mrs. Coffey led the South Carolina women in raising the funds for our first vehicle, a Rural Willys station wagon. Because of mission regulation we could purchase a vehicle only after the year of language studies.

December 14, 1960 rolled around quickly. With the necessary funds in our mission account, we, along with the Bobby and Sue Aycock, left for Brazil. O course, we had mixed emotions. It was not easy for us, a newlywed couple, to leave family, friends, and homeland, knowing it would be five years before we returned. But at the same time we felt peace in knowing we were in the center of God's will and would be under His protection and guidance.

Bobby's mother and one of his sisters came down to South Carolina the weekend before we left. That confirmed to me that Bobby's family was standing with us in the venture of God's will for our lives. That visit meant the world to Bobby and no less to me.

The night before we were to leave South Carolina, the Bobby Aycock family came by my parents' home on their way to Florida. They accepted an invitation to stay overnight. My parents were so gracious to give up their bed (and house) to be able to sleep the two missionary families. A neighbor took my parents in for the night. What a gesture of their love for the Lord's work on their part! Their sacrificial spirit showed that they were indeed supportive of Bobby and me in our decision to serve in Brazil and of others who would be serving as well. These acts of love brought to my mind my mother's words, "I had rather you go to Brazil with Bobby than to go to North Carolina with the last boy you dated." We had assurance that my parents believed we were God's choice for each other.

Bright and early the next morning, my mother was back in her kitchen getting a wonderful country breakfast for the crowd. That would be the last of her good homemade biscuits we would enjoy for five long years.

Not too long after the Aycocks left, Bobby and I put all our earthly belongings, which consisted of only our clothing and wedding presents, into my dad's car and headed off to Florida. We were on our way to the place of service God had given us.

Several of my cousins were living in the Miami area, so we went to Miami a couple of days early for a lovely visit.

My dad and mom took us to the airport. They had already decided that after the good-byes they would start back to South Carolina. The good-byes were especially difficult since we were still awaiting the call to board the plane. In fact, the plane could not get out of New York because of snow. Finally, though, my parents decided they should leave. Perhaps they thought it would be easier to leave us than to see us leave. I had an empty feeling when they left, as if I were losing something; but at the same time I felt that Bobby and I would be gaining more by doing God's will for our lives.

The airline put us up in the hotel at the airport for the night. Bobby's brother and his wife from Lakeland, Florida were there as well and decided to stay a little longer to go up to our hotel room to visit a while.

After Junior and Wilkie left, Bobby decided to go down to the lobby. Being the country boy he was, and also being young and needing to relieve some nervous energy, he decided to take the stairs. When he got to the bottom floor there was a sign on the door that read, "Do not open. Alarm will sound off." He went up to the first floor and tried to get into the hallway again, but found a locked door. He got his exercise as he climbed the stairs checking all the doors on the way back up. None of them would open for him. Finally, he reached the kitchen located on the tenth floor. There he met one of the cooks who said, "What you doing here. You can't come in here." Bobby asked, "How can a person get out of this place?" The cook then instructed, "You will have to go all the way back down to the bottom and open that door. It is your only way out."

Back down all those flights of stairs Bobby went. Getting to the bottom floor, he very easily opened the door and thought he was going to get out without the alarm going off, but he did not. When it did go off, it seemed that half of the workers in the hotel met him to keep him from getting into trouble with the airport police. From that point on, we've seen to it that we take the elevator when in a hotel.

The interesting thing about that experience was that, five years later, when we were back in the U.S. Bobby told his story. To his surprise, he found out that his brother and his wife had done the same thing. Everyone got a good laugh about that. It was a learning experience for those who were widening their horizons.

The next morning, December 14, 1960, Bobby and I, along with the Aycocks, boarded the 707 jet and were soon on our way to the giant country of Brazil. The 707 was the newest plane in service, but that did not keep these novices from being a little apprehensive about flying. Soon our nervousness was enhanced; we had left Miami and were out over the water. The plane was climbing at a normal rate. Then all of a sudden, it felt as if the plane were a fast elevator going down; it had hit an air pocket. After the sudden drop, it started climbing again and we knew things were fine. The interesting thing is that for a long time we expected a repeat, but it has never happened to us again.

Our first stop was in Panama. "Damas" and "Caballeros" were the words on the doors of the rest rooms. We had encountered our first problem with a foreign language. It only took a little observation to solve that problem and to add some new words to our vocabulary as well.

The second stop was in Ecuador, but we did not have to leave the plane. Leaving Ecuador, we were on our way to Lima, Peru. In Lima, we were told we had to disembark. All passengers were taken into an area and were locked in. It was a relief to be able to get back on the plane. The next stop would be Campinas, Brazil, our destination.

The Aycocks and the Pooles were the first missionaries to land at the new Viracopos airport in Campinas, Brazil. In fact, it was still under construction, so the plane stopped some distance from the terminal and the passengers had to walk quite a distance across an unpaved area. We were met in the terminal by all the Free Will Baptist missionaries on the

Brazil field, the Eagletons, the Wilkinsons, Dave Franks, Eula Mae Martin, and Esther Ruehle—plus another missionary who used her jeep to help take the two new families into town. The airport was about eight miles from the city, and the road was unpaved.

Things certainly were different. Getting into the city, we newcomers noticed that there were no display windows in the stores; or at least they appeared to have none, since all that we could see were large metal garage-type doors. Soon Bobby and I discovered that the display windows were only visible during the daytime when the stores were open, and at night these metal doors were pulled down to close off the view. Strange, is it not?

It was also soon evident to us that the driving rules in Brazil were quite different. At the street corner, even if there was a stop sign, all the driver did was blow the car horn during the daylight hours and blink the lights at night, then speed on through. Back in those days there was a limited number of cars, so people in the center of town stood out in the street to carry on their conversations. The cars had to dodge them.

§§

The words of the hymn, "Wherever He leads, I'll Go" by B.B. McKinney, took on a new meaning to us. Upon pondering on the words of that great hymn, we remembered the hymn referring to being drawn closer to Christ. The months of depending on God's mercy and grace, during our travels and raising funds, had indeed drawn us closer to our Lord. The hymn speaks of knowing the will of God. There was no doubt in our minds about the will of God. Yes, we were willing to go wherever He would lead.

03.
SETTLING IN

"As cold waters to a thirsty soul, so is good news from a far country." PROVERBS 25:25

Ken and Marvis Eagleton took Bobby and me under their wings to help us get settled, and Sam and June Wilkinson took the Aycocks into their home and care. Within about two weeks the duplex apartments that had been rented were ready and the basic furniture purchased, thus making it possible for both families to live side by side. Even though we had the help of each other, there were many things for both families to learn and many adjustments to make.

The daytime view of the city was also strange. People walked and used the trolley car or bus. There were so few cars for a city of two hundred and seventy thousand people. The age of the cars was astonishing in light of the new cars of the late fifties in the U.S. At that time, the only cars made in Brazil were the Volkswagen and Willys.

Soon the new missionaries learned that many food items were not available, such as mayonnaise, salad dressings, peanut butter, canned biscuits, and jellies. For me that was no big deal since others had made them before me, so I found recipes and went to work. Soon we found an *ENCYCLOPEDIC COOKBOOK*, which taught me how to do about everything, even to making apple butter. The things I could not learn to make, we would simply do without. Two other foods that we were unable to find were butter beans and peas (essentials to the South Carolinian diet), but I found plenty of substitutes.

The smells were certainly different and sometimes difficult to take. Bobby and I were reared in farm communities where our parents used, in most part, the things grown right there on the farm. Garlic was not among them. The garlic odor was repulsive to the sensitive nose of this young South Carolinian. I tried not to complain and tried not to get that wheezy feeling that came upon me with the strong smell of garlic cooking everywhere. It took some effort on my part, but a little thing like garlic was not going to destroy relationships or take me out of the country to which I came to serve the Lord. Finally, there was victory over the smell and the seasoning with garlic became a part of our daily lives. Until today I know the neighbor is preparing her beans, rice, and meat (all prepared with garlic), because that same smell comes around the corner and goes through the window into my kitchen. It is just a reminder that it is time to prepare a meal for my family.

The first Sunday in church, we will never forget. The seventeen people of the missionary family were loaded into the two, nine-passenger Volkswagen Kombi vans to make the thirty-minute trip across town to the house where the carport was being used as a meeting place. Naturally, all the newcomers had to go to the front to be introduced and say a word of greeting. First-time impressions of us expressed by the Brazilian Christians, to say the least, were interesting. The four were classified as handsome, intelligent, spiritual, and a doll. Size had a lot to do with the evaluation, since I weighed less than a hundred pounds and was low in stature, while the others were all tall by Brazilian standards.

Marvis needed some sewing done for the Christmas program at church. I jumped right in and helped many hours on these outfits. That was my first opportunity to be useful in relation to the church.

That first Christmas both families were still with their caregivers, but all the mission family had Christmas at the Eagletons. That day was a memorable one. Each person tried to make the new couples feel at home, loved, and accepted. Since the mission family had increased by six people, Marvis did not have enough dishes for everyone. Bobby and I dug around in our baggage and found our set of Melmac received from the campers in South Carolina as a wedding present. What an excellent way to break in these new dishes!

After we enjoyed a delicious meal, the group gathered in the living room to share the blessings of the Lord upon our lives. Bobby and I were elated to be present and wanted to give God the credit due Him for getting us to the field. I gave a short testimony expressing my thankfulness for the way God had moved in His perfect way—which did not mean we had no problems—during the three months of raising our support and bringing us safely to the field. One of the other missionaries laughed and said that he wished God had worked so perfectly for him. Nonetheless I was grateful we were all in God's place of service.

Some days before Christmas, Bobby and I, with paper and pencil in hand—and a few phrases we had learned in Portuguese, such as "Quanto é?" (How much does it cost?) and "Não falo português" (I do not speak Portuguese)—ventured out to catch a bus. We wanted to go to the center of town, do some shopping, and get back to the Eagleton's place again. We newlyweds had a great sense of adventure and enjoyed every minute of those activities.

§§

The rains seemed never to let up. *Rain, rain, go away* was in our thoughts and desires. We new missionaries were beginning to think it rained all the time in Brazil. It was raining the night we arrived in Campinas and continued to do so for more than two weeks. At least the temperature was a little more agreeable with the rains. When the sun popped out, the suffering began because of smoldering hot, humid temperatures. There were times that *Rain, rain, come again* were in our thoughts and desires.

We were learning another lesson. In Brazil, there is the rainy season during which it rains almost every day and sometimes weeks on end. Then there is the dry season during which time it rains very little for months. One year during those early days there was a period of seven months with no rain to speak about. Can you imagine the dust during the dry months? There was dust on the plants, the roofs, the floors, the tables. When the window shutters were opened to let the sunshine in, we discovered that the air was full of particles of dust. No wonder those who have allergy to dust have difficulty breathing.

The first week that Bobby and I were in Brazil, the men missionaries along with the Brazilian Christians installed the wiring for the electrical system in the church building. That was the last thing that had to be done before the new unfinished building could be occupied by the First Free Will Baptist Church in Brazil. Having finished that project, we attended our second Sunday school and services in the new building. During the year of 1961, that church became an intricate part of our lives and worship. Not knowing the language made worship a challenge.

The church started with a little group of believers whom Bro. Thomas Willey had contacted during his survey trip to Brazil three years earlier. After Dave Franks arrived, he also made contact with the group and it became the first Free Will Baptist church in Brazil.

An excerpt from the December 27, 1960 newsletter read, "We arrived in time to share the blessing of getting into the new church. Even though we could not understand the language, the first service was an impressive one. The service was on Christmas Eve. The program for the evening consisted of an ordination service for a young Brazilian preacher and then a Christmas program. Some of the people in the neighborhood did not want a protestant church in their neighborhood, so they threw small stones against the building. One stone crashed through a glass window where Bobby was standing. It is hard to explain just how we felt. We were not afraid; yet, our hearts went out to those who were trying to hinder the preaching of the Word."

Bobby and I enjoyed being with the Brazilian people. We enjoyed learning from them, but at times there were things difficult to swallow. For instance, the missionaries decided to go out to eat on one particular Sunday. I wanted to dress up a little more than the normal for church. Someone had already told me that Christians do not use the cross as jewelry or in their churches, mainly because of the Catholic Church. I felt the cross was a symbol of Christianity since it was not the crucifix; but in compliance with the Brazilian Christian's ideas, I kept my little gold cross in my jewelry box until it was lifted from that box and taken away by a thief a few years later. On that particular Sunday morning, I took out a string of tiny pearl beads to wear. No one said anything to me about the beads. The pastor called the missionary leader to the side and gave him instruction to have me not wear those beads anymore. The missionary told Bobby who waited until we got home to tell me. I cried, I prayed, I did not understand. The pastor himself used a gold tie clasp on most Sundays—at least it looked like gold. What was the difference? For the sake of the weaker brother, I gave up jewelry for a number of years. Of course, as the years passed, that pharisaical attitude did not continue to exist in the church in Brazil. Then some years later Bobby presented me with real pearls to wear.

During that first year, Bobby and I attended a missionary conference held at the New Tribes Bible Institute in Jacutinga, Minas Gerais.

Included in the fees for the conference were food and lodging. We stayed in a Salvation Army Children's Home. The first night there we almost froze. In that mountain climate the temperature drops and becomes rather cold during the winter months. One reason we were so cold was because there was a draft under the bed that felt like the air was coming up through the mattress onto our backs. Only one look at the mattress helped us recognize our problem. The mattresses (we were on single beds) were straw mattresses and the air was coming right through the straw. The next day we bought a newspaper and put a layer of paper under the mattresses and another between the top sheet and coverlet. We got more sleep the rest of the time there.

The meals were very simple. To be honest, they were a little difficult for me to eat because of the amount of garlic, but I did fine and Bobby really enjoyed them. I was adapting to the new surroundings. I admired Bobby for his acceptance of new and different things, and I tried hard to keep a good attitude as well.

As long as there have been Free Will Baptist missionaries in Brazil inflation has been a huge problem. Just before Bobby and I arrived in Brazil, a new money system became effective. The money was no longer "reis," but became the "conta." Some people, especially the older ones, were still referring to the money as "reis." After a number of years, the "conta" became the "cruzeiro." Then in a few years, the "cruzeiro" became the "novo cruzeiro," then after a period of inflation became the "cruzado." The "cruzado" became the "novo cruzado." The "novo cruzado" became the "cruzeiro" once again, and later the "cruzeiro" became the "real." All total, there have been eight or nine different money systems during the last fifty years. During some of those years, the inflation was as much as twelve percent per month. It does not take long until it is necessary to remove three zeros; thus, a thousand of the old would become a one in the new. It is rather confusing to say the least.

It is difficult for anyone who has not lived in a country where such high inflation takes place to realize the problems involved. For instance, when money is exchanged it is spent as soon as possible. There is no use in saving money because at the end of the month it has much less buying power. There is no way to teach children to save, because in a few months the money saved would have lost half of its value.

Bobby tells about the time he bought our first car, which cost about three thousand five hundred dollars. When he exchanged the money into the currency at the time, it filled up his briefcase, because the largest note was a 20 "contas." None of the missionaries had bank accounts at that time, so Bobby purchased the car with cash.

04.
LEARNING THE LANGUAGE AND CUSTOMS

"For thou bringest certain strange things to our ears: we would know therefore what these things mean." ACTS 17:20

How helpless not knowing the language made Bobby and me feel. In fact, not understanding the language made us feel as if we were outsiders and made it difficult to bond with the Brazilian people. We wanted so much to bond with them. Our newsletter of December 27, 1960, reads, "Our hearts hunger to be able to share the gospel of Christ. We long for the day when we can share the message with those around us each day."

It is impossible for anyone to settle into a country without learning the languages and customs of the country. Soon we faced that task when we started our studies at the Language and Orientation School.

At that time a larger number of missionaries had come into the country of Brazil; therefore, there were about thirty people, mostly Americans, in our class. We spent our first year learning new vocabulary, new sounds, and new customs. The letter *i* in Portuguese has the pronunciation of the long *e* in English. Unlike English, an *a* in Portuguese has only two sounds, *a* as in art and before the letters *n* or *m*, which has a nasal sound (as in under and umbrella). One pronunciation of the Portuguese *r* is like the English *h*.

Vocabulary was sometimes confusing. For example, if I used "entender" (understand) the person responding would normally use "compreender" (understand). I would often think, *I must have used the wrong word. I must remember it is not entender, but compreender.* Can you imagine that every word we knew in English we needed to learn an equivalent one in our new language? What a challenge that was for Bobby and me!

It is impossible to learn a new language without making quite a few errors; thus, we often said the wrong thing. While still in language school, Sue Aycock and I decided to stop by the corner store to buy some cookies. That happened during the days before we had learned that cookies were sold in grams of a kilo. Even if we had known, we did not know how to say "duzentos e cinquenta gramas" (two hundred and fifty grams). We decided we would ask for one-fourth of a kilo and that would solve our problem. We were not sure how to say "a fourth"; nevertheless, we practiced what we wanted to say. When we entered the store to make our purchase, the attendant did not understand a fourth of a kilo, but he understood four kilos (approximately nine pounds of cookies). We walked out with two bags of cookies. After it was all over, we had a good laugh at ourselves as we enjoyed the delicious little chocolate covered cookies.

Once while trying to give instruction to the girl helping me in the home, I told her to wash the walls of the street (estrada) when I meant the walls of the stairwell (escada). Evidently, she understood better than I was able to give instructions. Gestures may have been the secret.

One Sunday afternoon Bobby was preaching on the second coming of Christ. Waxing eloquently, he was giving some of the conditions that would exist in connection with the second coming of Christ. He meant to say, "Half of the people of the world will go to bed tonight with their stomachs (barrigas) empty." But instead he said, "Half of the world will go to bed tonight with their bladders (bexigas) empty." No one laughed. On the way home, I made the comment, "I know that all the mothers hope their children go to bed with their bladders empty." It was only then that Bobby realized he had made the error.

One Saturday, Eula Mae Martin, who worked with us for a few years, was going out to Luíz Antonio for a service. An oncoming car sped toward her with its lights on bright. With her fiancé in the car, she blurted out, "If you don't dim those lights I will 'give light' in your face." Actually what she said was that if he did not dim the lights she would give birth, have a baby, in his face.

We soon learned that all houses have fences or walls around them and between their yard and the sidewalk as well. The Brazilian considers the yard part of the house and no one is to enter without invitation. At the time Bobby and I arrived in Brazil, most houses did not have doorbells; therefore, the person desiring to enter stayed on the sidewalk and clapped his hands until someone answered the door.

It is a custom of the Brazilians, no matter how poor, to serve something to anyone making a visit in their home. It is also impolite to refuse whatever is being served. I wanted to do nothing to hinder relationships with the Brazilian people, so I did not refuse the coffee. To drink it would give me indigestion, so I invented ways to get rid of the coffee without being offensive. If the hostess left the room, I would exchange cups with Bobby. Once or twice the coffee went into a flower pot nearby. However, if I had to, I drank it and suffered later.

The Brazilian coffee is very, very strong and syrupy sweet. In fact, I have said that it is so strong and sweet that if the cup is turned upside down the coffee will stay in place like gelatin. Of course, that is an exaggeration, but it is definitely thick with sugar.

There are a number of old wives' tales or superstitions in Brazil which are hard to accept. Here are a few of them: A person will die if he drinks hot coffee and eats cold ice cream. A person must take his bath before the meal because he will die if he eats and then bathes. It is not good to eat food with black pepper because all the black pepper that enters the body will stick to the lining of the intestines and stay there.

There were many Brazilian gestures, which we needed to learn as well:
1. Execute GREETINGS with a handshake, then an embrace by placing hands on the forearms of the person being greeted; afterwards

cheeks touch on both sides as the air is kissed for a married person and three of these touching of cheeks for an unmarried person, so he/she will not have to live with his/her mother-in-law. "Boa noite" (good night) is the verbal greeting at night.
2. Express GOOD-BYES with a sideward wave of the open hand.
3. To express SHREWD or CLEVER, use the index finger to pull down the skin under one eye.
4. For NO or DO NOT DO THAT, put up the index finger and waves hand from side to side.
5. For DELICIOUS or EXCELLENT, the thumb and forefinger lightly grasp and shake the ear lobe, while the other three fingers are held open.

Short expressions called adages or well-known truths called proverbs are as small mirrors, which reflect the real meaning of a language. They are the voice of the people. The more the missionary learns to speak like the people, the more he is accepted. Here are some of the proverbs that Bobby and I have learned to use.

1. *O hábito não faz a monge.*
   Translation: The habit does not make the monk.
   American: Clothes do not make the man.
2. *Quem não tem cachorrro, caça com gato.*
   Translation: He who has no dog hunts with a cat.
   American: There is more than one way to skin a cat.
3. *Querer é poder.*
   Translation: To desire is to be able.
   American: Where there is a will there is a way.
4. *Filho de peixe, peixe é.*
   Translation: The son of a fish is a fish.
   American: Like father, like son.

Settling into the language takes much time and effort on the part of almost any missionary. For us, it took almost all of the first term of service to feel comfortable in our adopted language.

In the midst of learning the language, we wanted to be active. Opportunities arose for me to use my teaching abilities and experience. There were the Eagleton, Wilkinson, and Aycock children who were not getting formal Bible teaching in English. Once a week they all met at our house for me to give the children a Bible lesson in their first language. Those were precious times with the missionary children, who all called their teacher Aunt Geneva and do so still today.

Soon others in the language school heard about the English Bible class and really liked the idea. I formed a second class for children of other missionaries. The faces of these children are still vivid in my mind as I think back upon those precious times of teaching the Word to those little ones. Sometime I wonder what they are doing today and how they are spiritually.

In language school, the men went to school in the morning and the women went in the afternoon. The main purpose for that was so one parent could be at home with the children while the children made the necessary adjustments to their new surroundings, language, schools, etc. Since Bobby and I were married only three months when we arrived in Brazil, that separation was unnecessary, but was carried out since the school was set up on that fashion. That left Bobby at home most of the afternoon with nothing much to do except study the language. When he needed a break, he made his way to the kitchen where he enjoyed himself while making some kind of candy. His favorite kind was divinity. When the other missionaries came over he would serve his specialties. In fact, he became quite good at making divinity. Before all the missionaries moved out of Campinas to start their individual works, they had a coronation ceremony in which they bestowed upon Bobby an honorary "Doctor of Divinity" degree. That act spoke well of his divinity experience.

§§

From the very beginning, Bobby and I were faithful in the church in Campinas. Soon the Eagletons moved to the area near the church and the Wilkinsons to Jaboticabal. That left us with no mode of transportation available except the city bus system. The city bus was not ideal since we had to go to the center of the city and change buses to go out to the area of the church. The bus stop nearest to the church left a distance of about a mile uphill on a dirt street that became slick mud during the rainy season and powdery dust during the dry season. Sometimes Bobby and I had to hold to each other to keep from falling into the mud. Bobby and Sue Aycock and their two children were with us on these treks. Naturally, Bobby did his share of carrying the children. Many a time the whole group would laugh at each other in the predicament we found ourselves. All these trials were forgotten when we entered the church to worship God with the Brazilian people.

Worship was not easy for us because of the language. In the beginning, it seemed as if a complete sentence were only one long word. Then words we understood began to jump out and separate themselves from the rest of the sentence. Finally, sentences began to form. Naturally, that made things a whole lot better for learning and worship.

During that time, Bobby and I had opportunities to preach and teach occasionally. Of course, every word had to be written out and corrected by our language teachers. It was laborious but was a blessing to be able to be involved.

§§

The palm trees were swaying and drinking daily from the abundance of summer rain. The "natives" were beating on their drums and dancing wildly in the streets. It was not that Bobby and I were living out among uncivilized people. It was just the time of year of the Mardi Gras season, which in Brazil is called "Carnaval."

No sleep came to our eyes! Over on the opposite hill the samba band was preparing for the four nights of "Carnaval." The beat sounded satanic.

Brazil almost stops during "Carnaval." It is a time when Satan seems to be in control. It is also a time that reveals the depravity and desperation of the human heart. One of the large newspapers advertised on the front page in large letter, "Carnaval with many women, little clothing, and no happiness." Sometimes the pleasures of sin do not even last for a season.

For many good Brazilian Catholics, "Carnaval" is the last big fling before Lent. In general, the Brazilian lets his hair down, so to speak, and "lives it up" for the great celebration with dancing, drinking, drugs, nudity, sex, and all the base activities imaginable. The thought in the back of his mind is "Lent is coming," but that does not seem to hamper his indulging spirit.

"Carnaval" over, body and mind just do not want to function, but there is Ash Wednesday. On that day, forty days before Easter, the good Catholic makes his way into the cathedral, confesses his erroneous ways, says the number of prayers asked of him by the priest, gives alms and/or promises to abstain from a vice such as smoking or an amusement until after Holy Week. That is his time of penitence. With his conscience relieved, the cycle starts over again as he begins his preparation for next year's "Carnaval" event.

The heart or the way of life has not been changed, just inconvenienced a little!

§§

A newsletter written by Bobby in 1973 tells a little about that holiday. It reads:

"I was flabbergasted! 'Have a happy Carnaval' was what he said. There was no doubt about that, but I was speechless. I walked out of the store."

"Why should I have been speechless? For one thing, it was the first time anyone had wished me a happy 'Carnaval.' Then secondly, 'Carnaval' for the child of God represents the height of man's search for happiness outside of God. It actually reveals his depraved soul and the fruitlessness of his search. 'Carnaval' began this year on March 2 and ended sometime in the early morning hours of March 7. There were samba parades in the streets, but the main activities began around midnight in the clubs and halls scattered throughout the city. Hard drinks flowed freely and, of course, there was music—mainly the samba with its loud and famous beat which seems to tear down all inhibitions. Then, there were people, hundreds and sometimes thousands, packed on the dance floor and around the tables. Clothing was scarce, for both men and women. They danced (or 'jumped' as the Brazilians call it) on the tables, on the floor and even women riding the shoulders of their men partners, never missing the beat of the music. The frolicking continued until almost daybreak. Immorality is so prevalent that the birth of many children born out of wedlock dates from the time of 'Carnaval.' Have a happy 'Carnaval!' How? Playing the devil's game."

"The reason, then, for us being here in Brazil is to share with the Brazilian people the only true happiness, which is found in Jesus Christ by making Him Savior and Lord."

The outside world recognizes Brazil as a Catholic country, but there are more practicing Spiritists than there are practicing Catholics. In fact, in Brazil a person can be both a Spiritist and a Catholic. Having studied a little about the Catholic Church in Bible College, we understood a little more about Catholicism than we did about Spiritism. At least we knew that the Catholics put a false hope in the Virgin Mary, and emphases on the saints and the crucifix as well. With the forty days of lent over, the Catholics begin the activities of the Easter holiday which begins on the Sunday before Easter. The Catholic cathedrals are usually fuller on that Sunday with each person, carrying a palm branch, desiring to receive a blessing offered by the priest.

During the days before Holy Week, preparations are made for this important season. The long lines of those waiting to purchase dried codfish show the number who will practice the custom of eating only fish. The cathedrals are cleaned, ornaments polished, and statues made ready, including the glass encasement in which a statue of the body of Christ is placed. On Thursday night, certain areas of the Catholic churches are draped in black in final preparations for the big day on Friday.

Judas is also involved in their Easter celebration. Some people take a mannequin of Judas, usually homemade by stuffing an old pair of pants and an old shirt, and hanging him from a tree. The people pierce the mannequin with sticks and beat him showing their wrath for what he did to Jesus. Finally, in the late afternoon Judas is burned, getting rid of the one who caused Jesus so much suffering.

Good Friday comes! People are going into and coming out of the cathedrals! That first Easter season that we were in Ribeirão, Bobby and I went downtown to observe and to learn as much as we could about the way the Catholic celebrates Holy Week. We found that people kept entering and leaving the Catholic Cathedral. *Look!* I thought, *there is a person I have known for some time. Let's watch her.* With rosary in her hand, she is making her way into the church. As she passes through the door, she makes the sign of the cross. She walks a short way into the church, slips into a pew, where she kneels to say a few prayers using her rosary, and then just sits there as if she wonders what to do next.

Finally, she gets up and goes toward the altar of the church. We fix our eyes on a glass casket-like box in which has been placed a statue of the body of Christ that looks as if it has just been removed from the cross. My acquaintance has made her way to this casket. Yes, there are tears in her eyes, because she thinks, *Christ is dead.* She bends over and kisses the big toe, turns and walks away. As she leaves, her finger quickly wipes away a tear that had stopped on her cheek.

Leaving the cathedral, she again makes the sign of the cross, but her face is sad, with no hope expressed. In fact, Jesus is dead! Easter is over!

I thought to myself, *Can't you understand what I have told you about the victory of the resurrection?*

Easter Sunday came and went just like any other Sunday. In fact, the victory of the resurrection has no significance. To most of the Brazilian Catholics Jesus is still on the cross. They put the crucifix on chains abound their necks, on their walls, over their doors, in their places of business. How sad that they are so blind to the truth of the importance of the resurrection! They miss the new life that the resurrection offers!

For the Christian the triumph of Easter is glorious, but for the Brazilian Roman Catholic, Holy Week is just about the saddest time imaginable. Without the blessed hope, death is always sad!

One day Bobby and I went into a Catholic chapel for a wedding. As we entered, we were immediately impressed with the elaborately painted walls and ceilings, ornate scrolls, and inlaid gold. Many of the paintings reminded us of the stories we had learned in Sunday school.

Our eyes casually drifted to the mural painted in the dome at the front of the chapel. We could not believe what we saw. The false doctrine of the church boldly declared by the painting showed the place of prominence given to the Virgin Mary.

An old gray-haired man representing God, the Father, stood on the left. The young man standing on the right represented Jesus, the Son. The dove above the throne pictures the Holy Spirit. On the throne between the Father and the Son sat Mary, the "Mother of God" as some call her. God the Father and God the Son were placing a crown on Mary's head, crowning her as Queen of Heaven.

The director of the language school at that time was writing his doctoral dissertation on Brazilian spiritism. In the orientation class at the language school, he asked the students if they wanted to see firsthand what Spiritism was like. A group of the students decided to go with the director to a spiritist session. That was not the lowest type of spiritism, which places curses on people, but the kind that does good deeds for people. Among the group that went were the four Free Will Baptist missionaries who were in language school.

After the group of about ten missionaries entered the meeting hall, an usher separated us, the women sat on one side and the men on the other side. That meant that Sue Aycock and I were the only two missionaries on the women's side of the aisle. Much prayer had gone up before the encounter with the real worship of demonic powers.

During the meeting, no one could make any sign of the cross or even cross his legs or arms. The sign of the cross hindered in the receiving of the spirits. In fact, the leader said that they were having a hard time receiving the spirits. In spite of that, they continued singing and calling for the spirits to fall upon them. Finally, it happened.

All of a sudden, the circle of moving, chanting people stopped, when one member of the circle stopped, bent double at the waist with his head almost touching the floor and making a grunting, snorting sound almost like an angry hog. Soon that person fell to the floor rolling uncontrollably. Several people went to his assistance. Then it happened to others.

After getting the ones who were in a trance because they had received the spirits calmed down, they were taken and seated in a circle on the floor and given a pipe to smoke and a bowl of strong drink to sip occasionally.

As the incense burned, the odors changed in the hall. People from the audience went to the front. The leader met each person, directed him to one of the mediums and then had him sit on the floor in front of the medium who would serve him. There was low mumbling and then the work began as the person in the trance began his work moving his trembling hands in the air over the head and shoulders of the one he was helping, by performing a healing, casting out an evil spirit, or keeping an enemy from working against him, his family, or his business.

As we missionaries witnessed the satanic control, sadness fell upon each of us. We left the meeting with a renewed desire to help people leave their walk of darkness and come to the true Light, Jesus. In general, false teachings easily deceive the Brazilian people.

On another occasion, a group from the language school went to a session of the Alan Kardec followers. That type is known as the white table spiritism. In that session, those aspiring to be enlightened or speak with a dead loved one or used by a spirit to help others were seated around a long white table. The session started with a Bible study. In that particular session, the study text was John 14:2: "In my father's house are many mansions." The teacher said that the many mansions refer to the seven spheres of reincarnation. Each person has to pass through the seven realms of reincarnation before he reaches the perfect and ultimate sphere called heaven. He also said the way to receive reincarnation into a higher sphere is to follow the example of Jesus and do good works. Jesus is the example! Jesus set that example of doing good works while He was here on earth. The more the spiritist works and the more good he does, the better chance he has of not returning to the same level or sphere in his next reincarnation, but going to a higher one which is a little closer to the ultimate sphere.

Also, in the study, he used the words "be born again" found in John 3:3 and 7 as proof of the different reincarnations. A person has to be reborn and reborn until he finally reaches the ultimate sphere, heaven.

How sad it was for us to come to a realization of how many people are involved in that type of error. Our job given to us by God is to present the truth, to bring those walking in darkness unto the Light.

Bobby and I have seen things, which have taught us much about demon worship.

An experience that struck us most profoundly perhaps was a trip up to the famous statue of Christ, the Redeemer, on the Corcovado Mountain in the city of Rio de Janeiro. The statue, with arms outstretched placed on the mountain above the bay and city, is a visible sign that Christ is calling people to accept Him. The statue is visible from miles away from most any part of Rio. The sky was relatively clear, so between passing clouds we took a number of pictures. Down below the precipice of the mountain was one of the many favelas (shantytowns) where the unskilled, uneducated, and unemployed had put together with whatever materials he could find a shanty in which to live with his large family. Middle-class homes, factories, business districts, skyscrapers, beautiful hotels, and apartment buildings along the Atlantic Ocean, as it rolled into the white sands of the Botafogo and Copacabana beaches, along with the famous Sugar Loaf Mountain, could be viewed from the mountain top.

Bobby and I, along with another missionary couple, chose the old back road to make our decent down the mountain. On the road, we saw something that made the deepest impression upon each of us. It was the remains of a Macumba session. Macumba, widespread throughout Brazil, is a fetish ceremony of African origin with Christian inflection, accompanied by dances, songs, drums, sorcery, and witchcraft.

We four missionaries came upon a small clearing where we stopped the car to investigate. A number of clay bowls were scattered around; some were broken, some turned upside down, others upright, still others almost covered with pieces of bright red and dull black cloth which represented blood and death or curse. There were partially decayed goat heads, black chickens, bones and blood from sacrificed animals, and manioc flour mixed with blood, as well as candle wax and match stems everywhere. Near the center of the clearing, we found a number of quart bottles that were filled with alcohol, and each contained a piece of paper on which was just scribbling and a name or names of individuals to be recipient of the curse.

We found two cloth dolls stitched together face to face. Straight pins pierced their heads and bodies where vital organs should be. These evidently represented a man and woman, possibly lovers or a married couple. The objective was to invoke the evil spirits to either kill or physically harm those they represented.

Learning more about demon worship, we were more determined to do all possible to preach salvation through the death, burial, and resurrection of the Lord Jesus Christ.

One day Bobby and I heard about the "barbeiros" in our area of Brazil. We learned that the little bug, which looked much like a small roach with a pointed head, was very harmful. When one of these little bugs infected with the "chagas" virus bites a person, he becomes infected with the virus, which can stay dormant for years or can pop up anytime to cause heart problems. The virus causes the muscles of the heart to harden, which in turn causes death.

Not long after hearing of the dreaded little creature, Bobby was on his way home from a service in a small town near Ribeirão Preto. He noticed a person who had fallen on the side of the road. He stopped to see if he could be of help. He learned that the person was walking and fell over dead. A doctor also stopped. He said the death was no doubt the consequences of the disease.

Perhaps when we first heard about the dreaded little creature we were a little preoccupied about becoming victims. God's Word says, "be careful for nothing" (Philippians 4:6), which spoke to our hearts. Our trust in God to take care of His own soon removed that worry. Our great desire was to continue in the work and get the most done for Christ.

As the years have gone by, a precaution lingers about the "barbeiros." From time to time, we hear of someone who has died from "chargas" disease caused from a bite of the "barbeiro." We have known and still know a number of people who have the disease. Our closest neighbor, who is a Christian, has that type of heart problem. One of my English students from 1970, who came to know the Lord, has the disease as well. In fact, just recently a cardiac physiotherapist said "chagas" affects the majority of her patients.

Missionaries soon learn that things do not move very quickly in Brazil. For instance, Bobby had to go down to the water department six times before he eventually got the water connected at our building site.

It seems there is a line to wait in to get anything done. Times of waiting are very trying. For instance, when we returned to Brazil after our first furlough, we sold our old car and purchased another one. We had to wait two weeks before we could get the new car. Then we received only a five-day permit to drive the car while we got permanent license plates. When the five days ran out we still had not been able to get the license plates, so for five more days the car sat in front of our house resting while Bobby and I walked.

The problem of waiting is always present. We have been trying to wade through the process for approval for construction of the church building in Marincek. The process has already drawn out to more than three years. Finally, during the first part of September 2009, we received the approved plans. On that very day, another engineer received the plans to do the structural calculations. October came and was quickly passing without calculations in hand. Dates set to receive the calculations came and went. A person's word is no guarantee. Finally, on the very last day of October we received the important paperwork.

§§

Most of the river waters of Brazil have the bloodthirsty piranha fish in them. These little fish, ranging from four to eighteen inches in size, are considered more dangerous than the shark. Thousands of them sometimes travel in schools. These fish have been known to tear, with their razor-sharp teeth, all the flesh off the skeleton of an animal or a human being in only a few minutes.

At places along the rivers, there are cattle ranches. Sometimes it is necessary to take the cattle from one side of the river to the other. No bridges and the presence of the piranha fish are real problems.

One solution is a sacrifice. The cattlemen choose one of the cows, take it up stream, slaughter it and throw it into the water. The blood of the cow draws the piranhas in that direction. While the fish pull the flesh, bite by bite, from the bones of that cow, the cattlemen quickly take the rest of the herd across the river. One cow is sacrificed to save the whole herd.

That story brought to my mind I Corinthians 5:7: "For even Christ our Passover is sacrificed for us," and has given to our hearts a greater desire to share this message.

§§

We missionary do not know why, whether it is to please or to save face, but the Brazilian usually will say what he thinks the person who is dealing with him wants to hear. For example, he will declare he is going to church on Sunday, when he does not intend to fulfill his word. He will listen to a gospel presentation and even go through the motions of accepting Christ, but in reality it is only a formality. It seems as if there is a hard shell around his heart, or perhaps like the Brazil nut two of them. How sad!

The Brazil nut comes from a large tree that grows in the rain forest near the Amazon River and its tributaries. This straight tree grows up to one hundred fifty feet tall with a base up to six feet in diameter. Its wavy leaves are bright green and often grow fifteen inches long and six inches wide.

The tree is not important for its size, wood, or magnificence, but for the delicious nut, the seed. The nuts form inside a round, almost coconut-shaped woody hull. Each hard hull has from twelve to twenty-five nuts, or hard-shelled kernels. It is not easy to open the one-fourth inch, hard shell to get down to the hard shell of the nut as known to the world.

The nut gatherers hammer away to break the shells to be able to furnish the tasty nut. We continue our work at chipping away the hard shell of customs and traditions by presenting the true gospel until the hardened heart cracks open and another person is reached for Christ.

§§

Weddings are certainly unique in Brazil. First of all, the attendants at a wedding are called godparents, and are usually married couples already established in life. The bride and the groom choose several couples to stand with them in their wedding. During the ceremony, these couples are standing on both sides of the minister almost forming a semicircle. The parents of the bride and groom make up the semicircle as well. Photographers are a great distraction. They do not do their work discretely.

When the person officiating pronounces the couple as husband and wife, the groom goes first to the godparents of the bride to compliment them while the bride goes to the godparents of the groom. Each then goes on to compliment their own godparents. Wedding gifts from the godparents are gifts such as a stove, refrigerator, china, silverware, etc. to get them off to a good start in setting up housekeeping. According to Brazilian customs, the groom's parents help with the couple's furniture, while the bride's parents pay for the wedding.

Status is involved in bringing about some of the wedding customs. Most of the time, the wedding invitation includes an invitation to the wedding dinner. For instance, when our son John and Renata were married, Renata's father gave a dinner in a nice restaurant for two hundred and eighty-five guests.

Another interesting thing is that, as the meal is about to come to an end, friends of the groom will take the groom's tie and go from table to table cutting off a piece of it for each person who gives a monetary gift. This gesture gives the newlyweds a little extra cash for their honeymoon.

Funerals are also quite different in Brazil. There is no pomp and ceremony. The burial takes place within twenty-four hours of the death in quite an informal way.

The casket is so different. It is narrow at the ends and wider at about where the shoulders are, to allow the body to fit into the casket. The whole top of the casket comes off; thus, a cloth covers the body from the waist down and usually on top of the coverlet, flowers are placed as well. Embalming is virtually not done except with permission in very rare cases.

Most of the time the body "lies in wake" at the funeral home in a small room with about twenty chairs. If there is any kind of funeral service, everyone present tries to gather into the room to hear the few words spoken. At the appointed time, the funeral home attendant takes the body to the cemetery. While the people are just standing around, someone, perhaps a member of the family, says a few words. Then with the use of old, dirty ropes, workers lower the casket into the underground tomb and place it on one of the shelves. As everyone stands there looking on, a worker closes the shelf off with rough brick and mortar and then closes the tomb by sliding the concrete slab back over the top opening. That is the signal for everyone to leave. Definitely, there is no pomp and ceremony.

Flowers are not a big thing at a funeral in Brazil. Even today, a couple of flower wreaths and two or three potted plants are all that will be the part of the funeral.

If the burial is of a Catholic or a Spiritist, there is a lot of wailing and lamentations, and often a person or two faints. This seldom happens at a Christian funeral. However, it does occasionally, if a family member regrets the way he had treated the deceased. The Christians show the blessed hope they have in the Lord Jesus.

The smallest insect, the largest animal, and any living creatures in between are called "bichos," and there are a lot of them in Brazil.

One day I was going about my business of washing dishes. As usual, I was involved in my own thoughts when suddenly my attention was drawn to a buzzing sound, first outside the window and then slowly getting louder inside the kitchen. I was amazed and somewhat alarmed at the number of blowflies swarming outside the window. I was even more amazed at their ability to find an opening around the screened window and work their way in. With the spray and a fly swatter, I managed to eliminate scores of the greenish little creatures.

Back to the sink, I still could not get my mind off that tiny insect which can be such a nuisance. Ecclesiastes 10:1 popped into my memory: "Dead flies cause the ointment of the apothecary to send forth a stinking savour: so doth a little folly him that is in reputation for wisdom and honour." My thoughts made the comparison using perfume to wisdom and dead flies to foolishness.

Then I remembered Ephesians 5:2, which give me the command to "walk in love, as Christ . . . an offering and a sacrifice to God for a sweet smelling savor [fragrant aroma]." The expression "fragrant aroma" comes from the Old Testament. The offering of a sacrifice became a fragrant aroma acceptable to God. Then I remembered the children's story about becoming a perfume for Christ in which II Corinthians 2:15 is the key scripture verse. This verse tells me that not only am I to be perfume to saved people, but to perishing ones as well.

 I then asked myself if I had always spread a fragrance pleasing to God. That day I accepted the challenge to refine my Christian character so that I would shed a delicate aroma for Christ to those whom my life touches.

05.
INTO THE WORK

"Wherefore we receiving a kingdom which cannot be moved, let us have grace, whereby we may serve God acceptably with reverence and godly fear." HEBREWS 12:28

"Indians in Brazil need Christ" were the words on our first prayer card. We knew more about the needs of the Indian work because of information received from New Tribes Mission and Wycliffe Bible Translators than we did of the needs in other parts of Brazil. The logical thing was to respond in that direction through the knowledge we had acquired. We went to Brazil to work in some remote Indian village.

While we were in language school, a missionary couple who was working in one of the tribes contacted us. They had to leave their post of ministry, and they were looking for a replacement. Our spirits were high as we made plans to visit the Indian tribe during the days off from our language studies, but we had to cancel the trip because of an upheaval in Brazil's government after the president resigned.

With our formal language training about to terminate, we began searching for a place to begin a work. We had come to Brazil to work among the Indians, but at that very time the government Indian Protective Service would not allow anyone new into the Indians tribes. We realized also that we were unprepared to face the linguistic side of Indian work, so we turned our eyes in another direction.

We made several weekend trips to search for the right place. We wanted God to direct us, and we humbly asked His direction as we looked at a map of the state of São Paulo. This was where the missionaries on the field had decided to expand the Free Will Baptist work. Bobby sensed that Ribeirão Preto was the place. He said it seemed that the name Ribeirão Preto lit up like a neon light as he studied the map. On our very first trip to the city, we felt a confirmation that Ribeirão Preto was God's place of service. This was a city of one hundred and twenty thousand, which we called our concrete jungle.

As soon as we were certain about the place, the search for a house began. Our faith was tested when we were unable to find a suitable house and the weeks kept rolling by. We even decided that perhaps we should pursue another place, so on our way back to Campinas we stopped in the smaller town of Porto Ferreira to check the possibilities there. Several hours of searching led to no avail. On the next trip, we went back to Ribeirão Preto.

Dave Franks, Bobby, and I rode the streets looking for a place to live. Dave was to work along with us for three months until he left for furlough. We passed a "For Rent" sign on a two-story house that people were entering. We stopped just to ask about the house. The woman who was also searching for a house to rent kindly invited us to go though the house with her. We decided upon seeing the place that we would take it if the person ahead of us did not rent it. We contacted the owner to express our interest in the house. The owner was to give us an answer the next day. What a relief it was to learn the house was available! We had rented our first place in the city of Ribeirão Preto.

One day Bobby went into a bakery at the same time the person entered who allowed us to look at the house with her. They started talking. She asked where he was living. He told her we had rented the house we looked at with her. She explained to him that the owner did not want to rent to anyone with five children, therefore, she did not get the house.

An excerpt from our February 13, 1962, newsletter read, "We have so much for which to praise the Lord. Within the last eight days we received our Rural Willys station wagon and also rented a house. During that time, we also received our drum of books that had been in the seaport of Santos for over a year. Renting the house on Wednesday, leaving only one day to pack, we decided to move on Friday. By 8:00 Friday night (February 9,

1962) we had moved. That Saturday afternoon we left for Jaboticabal to help in a weekend conference."

※

While working on the things required in beginning a new work, we decided to make a survey of the area around Ribeirão Preto.

Winding down the farm road on a Sunday in February of 1962, before the work in Ribeirão Preto was started, Bobby and I, along with Dave Franks made our first visit to the little farm village of Albertina. In the small town of Dumont, a person told us about a Christian who lived in Albertina. We headed off to the farm village in search of that Christian, but as it turned out the person was a spiritist. As we rode along the bumpy road, all three of us silently prayed not only for the working of the Holy Spirit, but also that it would not rain until after our return trip—for we knew the road would be impassable after a rain. The people were friendly. We asked if we could sing a few songs that spoke about God and give them a short message. Without reluctance, they gave us an invitation to return.

The first year we returned about every Wednesday night for an open-air meeting with no visible results; no one had stepped out accepting Christ as personal Savior. The people would say, "We want you to come. We like the music, the message, and the film strips, but we just do not understand." Even after a year, we did not give up. We continued leaving the people with the message and praying that the Holy Spirit would teach them the truth.

※

In April of 1962, we began a Sunday school with children eager to hear the Bible stories, which we told using flannelgraph and other helps. On some Sundays, there were as many as 50 children present. Of course, many adults stood in windows and doorways and sat on steps listening to the Bible lesson.

Then real trouble began. The public school teacher told the children that if they attended the Sunday school she would not let them continue studying in the village school, which had nothing to do with the Sunday activities; however, most of them believed her. She also encouraged a few demonstrations.

One Wednesday night someone put nails under the tires of our vehicle and someone else removed them. Rocks were piled in the road to block it; therefore, we had to remove them before we could continue. There was talk among some of the people about stoning us the next time we were there. Later we learned that a man who was friendly to us and to the work we were doing carried a gun for our protection.

One night more than a hundred people were watching a filmstrip, powered off the car battery since the village had no electricity. I remember how several men who were riding fast on horses came toward the assembled group shouting, "Cows, Cows." Naturally, the group scattered.

Since Brazil has religious freedom and we have permanent visas, we have the same rights as Brazilian citizens. Bobby decided it was time for him to go to the Educational Department and make a complaint. It got results. Soon that teacher was replaced, but much damage had already been done.

※

Bobby and I were beginning to wonder if the gospel would ever penetrate the hearts of the people in the village of Albertina. We slowly began to recognize that the greatest enemies were ignorance, fear, and superstition. The people remained in ignorance because they believed the priest who told them the missionaries were using the Bible and no one was to read or interpret the Bible except the priest. Their fears continued because they were taught that the Catholic Church is the only way to get to heaven. Their superstitious nature caused them to not do anything that might be against the traditions they had been taught.

In February of 1963, our hearts were overjoyed to see one of the men, Ferminio, step out for Christ during the invitation. Ferminio was faithful to the Lord and to those who led him to the Lord even in our most unpopular days. Soon after his decision, twelve others accepted Christ as Savior.

Among those saved was Dona Tereza. She had the title, "Mother of the Village" since she was midwife, nurse, and spiritual counselor for the vast majority of the people. She was in charge of the small Catholic chapel and was responsible for caring for the priest when he came. She was also in charge of collecting the alms, penitence, and offering for the church. The people were obligated to give a certain amount each year. When the people did not give, Dona Tereza made up the difference. It was a difficult decision for Dona Tereza to turn her back on Catholicism. For a while, she tried to serve the two; she did not want to give up either. Nevertheless, after some months she realized the truth and stepped out by faith, leaving her Catholic practices behind. She encouraged others to buy a Bible and get into the Word. Her testimony was that God had touched her body and her heart as well.

It was a religious desire that generated the beginning of Ribeirão Preto. In 1856 the first small chapel, São Sabastião, was built so the inhabitants of a vast region could have religious assistance. The chapel was located between the creeks Retiro and Ribeirão Preto on land donated by a farmer in the area.

As time and people came and went, around the chapel a village was developing. By 1874 the first election for city officers was held, giving the town the name "Entre Rios" (Between Rivers), and by 1883 the railroad had reached the village. The name was changed in 1889 to the name it still bears today: Ribeirão Preto (Black River).

It was also a religious desire that generated the beginning of Free Will Baptists in Ribeirão Preto. By 1962, when Free Will Baptists entered the city, the population measured approximately 120,000, with a few small churches scattered about the center of the city. Certainly, there was a great need to reach Ribeirão Preto for Christ. We wanted to be used to help reach them.

The need of reaching these masses burned in the heart of Bobby from his very first survey visit to the city. I was there by his side wanting to be a help in doing what God led him to do.

Missionaries with a vision, with stamina, and with a desire to reach the Brazilian people for Christ caused Bobby and me, along with Dave Franks, to get busy with the work.

The first big question after settling in Ribeirão Preto was, "How is a church started from scratch?" We did not know a single Christian who would become a part of the work.

The method chosen to begin the work was to rent a meeting place, furnish it with a few homemade benches and a rostrum, and start with a Sunday school in the morning and a campaign of eight nightly services beginning on Sunday night.

Bobby and Dave canvassed the area, trying to meet as many people as possible to talk to them about the new church we were starting and to leave a printed gospel message with them. We did not discover a single Christian in the area we had chosen to begin the work.

Five weeks after moving to Ribeirão Preto the meeting hall was ready, and tracks, gospel portions, and invitations were already in the hands of the people in the area. These invitations gave them information about a Sunday school hour on Sunday, March 11, 1962, and a week of meetings beginning on that same day, going through the following Sunday, March 18. Dave Franks did the preaching each night. Sam and June Wilkinson came from Jaboticabal to help with the music. Bobby and I did the teaching in the Sunday school. God used His Word because by the second Sunday many of the same people returned to the Sunday school hour, as well as a number of new people. Even though people of the black book were not very well accepted, to our delight sixteen people were present for that first Sunday school. The work in Ribeirão Preto had its beginning.

To begin the work we were able to find only a one-room hall to rent, which made conditions that were not ideal. At first, we did not even have a rest room. Nevertheless, it was a start. We started with our Sunday school completely departmentalized. Everyone was in the same department, same class, and same teacher. Everyone from babies to grey-haired adults sang, prayed, and listened to the flannelgraph stories. After all, they were all on the same level as far as Bible knowledge was concerned.

Any Sunday school authority would say right off that these conditions are not ideal for growth, and, of course, they are one hundred percent right. Bobby and I tried to divide the Sunday school by putting benches outside for the older people, but the noise was so great we soon abandoned the idea and the students returned to the hall. We continued that way for about six months. During that time, the attendance grew to an average of thirty. Then the Lord provided the much-needed space. One of the neighbors moved and that house became available. That was a precious answer to prayer.

There were no funds available from the mission for the hall, the furnishings, or the rented house for us to begin the new work. From the very beginning, we learned to trust the Lord for the financial needs of the work in Ribeirão Preto. God built strong, self-supporting Free Will Baptist churches in this city to the glory of His grace.

On May 17, 1964, with sixteen charter members, the First Free Will Baptist Church of Ribeirão Preto was officially organized. Our small group had a desire to push forward with evangelistic efforts to build a church for Christ's glory.

As always, when the gospel begins to penetrate, the devil tries his best to stop the progress. During the first four years, the church had three different meeting places and none of those places with their drab storefront appearance presented a positive picture for the gospel. While in the second meeting hall, the Sunday school attendance reached one hundred and five, but there was no way possible to teach and keep that number with such little space available.

One day Bobby observed a newcomer to the service. He also observed that the man was singing the hymns and participating in the service, which is unusual for a newcomer. After the service, Bobby talked to the visitor. He found out that he was in town because of his work. He was a representative for a firm and was in town on business.

Bobby asked him if he would like a visit. He gave Bobby his name and the boarding house where he was staying, and a visit was set for a day or so later.

When Bobby arrived, he went to the room where José said he would be. He knocked, but no one came to the door. Bobby did not give up. He continued knocking. Finally, José came to the door. He did not seem too happy at first to see the pastor, but he did invite Bobby into his room. He began telling Bobby about his life. He had been a Baptist pastor in the state of Goiás. How sad it was to hear how he had fallen into sin when he became involved with a member of the church. That brought about separation from his wife.

Then he told Bobby that he was at rope's end and when he heard the knock at the door, he was standing in front of the mirror contemplating suicide. Bobby showed him from the Bible that God still loved him and talked to him about his need to repent and allow God to work in him. Before Bobby left, he knelt beside his bed, repented of all he had done, and asked God to forgive him. He really seemed to be sincere. A second visit was set for a few days later. When Bobby returned, he got no answer to his knocking. He received information that the person who had occupied that room had left, therefore, all contact with him was lost.

Some years later Dona Maria, a woman from Goiás, came to Ribeirão Preto to live with her daughter. That dear Christian woman was a blessing to our church. Every once in a while she would go back to Goiás for a short time.

After one of these visits she shared the following story with Bobby and me. She had gone into the interior of the state to visit with relatives. One Sunday she had visited a small Baptist Church near the relatives' home. The pastor recognized her as a visitor and asked her where she was from. She gave Ribeirão Preto and her church as the Free Will Baptist Church.

As soon as the service ended, the pastor made a beeline to her. He asked, "Did you say you are from the Free Will Baptist Church in Ribeirão Preto?" After a positive reply, he asked her if Pastor Bobby was her pastor. Then he gave her his story of what had happened to him and asked her to give a message to Pastor Bobby. He asked her to tell Bobby that, because of his visit, he had gotten his life right with God, gone back to Goiás, and had gotten things right with his wife and with the church as well. By that point, God had already used him as an instrument to begin two churches.

What a blessing to learn what had taken place and to be a small part of God's overall work!

§§

Bobby and I, along with our young son Robert, lived in a house on the corner of the streets José da Silva and Carlos Chargas during the last half of our first term of service in Brazil. One day we heard a crash on the corner of the two streets. Soon we discovered that a little three-wheel car had turned the corner and ran into our Rural Willys station wagon.

Of course, Bobby ran out to see if anyone was hurt. The only person in the car was a seventeen-year-old who did not have a driver's license. He begged Bobby not to call the police and said that he would pay the damage, which was minor to the station wagon. His little car suffered much more damage.

That day was an opportunity. We invited Antonio to go to the youth meeting on Saturday night. Perhaps out of courtesy or because we were Americans, he went to the youth meeting on that Saturday night and to a few others as well. Antonio lived some distance from the church in another part of the city. He learned of a small church that had opened much nearer his home, so he started attending that church.

A few years latter, he married a Christian girl. They were forming a Christian home when tragedy struck. Antonio's wife died when their third child was born. That tragic event did not destroy his faith; it strengthened it, but his life had suffered a tremendous blow. Of course, his family helped him, and the church family did as well. After a few years, he married the pastor's daughter who became a mother to his children. He has been a stalwart testimony of the glory of Christ's grace.

Every now and then, Bobby and I still cross paths with Antonio. We remember the way we met and how it turned out to be a blessing.

§§

Bobby and I had made a contact with a group of people who lived not far from the meeting hall in a village called Cateto. The contact came about through a young girl who liked the music and, out of curiosity, came into the hall one night during the service. Through Rosária we got to know several families, and many in these families came to know the Lord and began attending church.

One Sunday in late 1964, we will always remember as a day full of tragedy. When the students were returning from their classes to enter the meeting hall, one of the newcomers, Graci, tripped and fell. It would not have been so bad, but she already had a brace on her leg because she was suffering from a bone infection called osteomylitis. Bobby took her, along with her mother, to get her leg checked out. It was broken, which was very serious with her existing problem.

I took charge of the closing out of the Sunday school assembly. Sr. José, who lived in the house connected to the rented hall and Sunday school classrooms, was a Christian and a member of the church. When he locked the meeting hall, Robert and I had no place to go since I had not taken my house key with me; therefore, he and his wife invited us to their house. I was thankful for a place to stay out of the hot sunshine.

Sr. José decided to make coffee. He boiled the water in an electric pitcher. Then he put in the coffee grounds and stirred the coffee. Naturally, our two-year-old son wanted to see the operation, so he stood right next to Sr. José. Katarina, his daughter, came by and hit his arm, jerking it and causing the hot coffee and grounds to fall directly on Robert's head. There were coffee grounds in his eyes, his ears, and all over his head. Someone grabbed an egg and I applied it as quickly as possible. Sr. José wanted to know where I wanted to take him. I knew Bobby had taken Graci to the city emergency room, so off we went. Bobby was still there, so we let the doctor on duty check Robert, but we were not satisfied. When we got home, we put Foille, a medicine for burns, on his face and neck, in his ears, and close to his eyes. After doing that, we called the pediatrician we always used, Dr. Scatena, who said that the medicine we used was the best. If blisters came up near his eyes or Robert started having fever, we were to call the doctor immediately; but if things went well, we should take him to his office the next morning. When the doctor saw him, he said that it was a miracle that his burns were no worse. In fact, Robert has no permanent scars. His fever, which had started during the night, was from a sore throat—probably from screaming so much.

Graci's story did not turn out so well. She had to have surgery and stay in a cast for months. That did not hinder the family's quest for learning more about the true and living God. At least two or three members of her family were at church every time the doors were open.

After years of suffering and twenty-plus surgeries, Graci lost that leg. Through help from Samaritan's Purse, she was able to get a mechanical leg and continued serving the Lord. All her problems, however, had put a strain on her heart, and she went home to be with the Lord when she was only in her thirties.

One of the most promising young lads in the church was Luiz. He had a quick mind and could easily memorize Scriptures. When he was ten years old, he accepted Christ. Everyone liked him; he made friends easily.

His father had died when he was a tiny tot, therefore, he did not have a father image in the home. During his teenage years, he became difficult to deal with. Once he ran away from home and ended up in the seaport town of Santos, about 250 miles from Ribeirão Preto. After discovering where he was, Bobby went down and convinced him to come back to Ribeirão Preto with him.

Luiz remained unhappy; he always looked for adventure. At that time, in the central Square of Ribeirão, several young people very well indoctrinated into the "Children of God" movement were looking for other young people to entice. These young people intrigued Luiz and he began hanging around the square. Before he was hardly aware of what was going on, these young people had convinced him to go to their training camp in Rio de Janeiro.

Once again, without his mother knowing about it, he was off for another experience. What an experience that camp entailed! In the first place, he had to give up his documents. He was assigned a personal monitor and counselor. That person had the responsibility of being with Luiz twenty-four hours a day; thus, Luiz could never be alone. All the teaching and conversation done were for the sole purpose of brainwashing him into an acceptance of the false doctrine.

Finally, Luiz recognized what was going on. He succeeded in leaving the encampment and made his way back to Ribeirão Preto, even without documents.

The saddest part of this story is that even though on several occasions we have succeeded in getting Luiz to go to church, he is yet a confused person that has never recovered from his rebellious years.

If only Luiz had trusted God for victory, he would be a man of God today.

Graci and Luiz had a saintly mother who served the Lord for many years as a Sunday school teacher in the Free Will Baptist Church. Only after she moved too far away to get to participate did she find her a church group near where she lived.

Dona Benê had two other children. Benedito had made a decision for Christ and stayed faithful in attendance in the Free Will Baptist church until he married. His is a sad situation. He dropped out of church because he married into a Spiritist family and would not buck the tide.

Marlene was faithful in church, but seemed to be attracted to friends who led her to do things that showed her wild side. Her mother was concerned. Bobby and I visited the family on many occasions, but, seemingly, our counsel went unheeded.

One night that saintly mother was very concerned for her daughter, who had started going out with a married man. She went into her bedroom and poured her heart out to the Lord. As she remained on her knees, she shed tears and begged God to stop the relationship before Marlene totally turned her back on the Lord. She told God that she knew Marlene was still a Christian and that she did not want her to lose her faith. She asked God to do whatever He needed to do to stop her. Within a few days, Marlene was out riding around in a car with that friend. The car ran off an overpass and caught on fire. Both were victims of death by fire. We may say, "What a tragedy!" But that precious mother said something like this: "I thank the Lord for taking Marlene before she completely turned her back on the Lord and lost her salvation. I believe she is in heaven now."

It had not been an easy road to get a church started with the struggles of learning a language; however, our first term of service was quickly ending. None of the church people wanted us to leave. The new Christians shed many tears during the last service. Our parting was even more difficult because we did not expect to return to that church and these people.

The group of believers needed a leader, so Sam and June Wilkinson went to Ribeirão Preto to lead the church. However, to our surprise upon our return to Brazil, we were given permission to return to Ribeirão Preto and the Wilkinsons to go to the campground near Jaboticabal, where they had already served.

Stateside assignment is always a rather stressful time. Closing down shop on the field and opening up shop again in the U.S. takes much planning, consumes much energy, and emotionally requires much of the missionaries. Bobby and I are thankful for the blessing of never having to rent a house in the states. Until the death of my mother in 1988, my parents' home on the family farm in South Carolina became our home. Naturally, our boys enjoyed not only the farm life, but also getting to know their grandparents—and making memories that have continued to live on in their minds and hearts. Granddaddy Hicks always had time for his grandchildren, loved them, played with them, laughed with them, went places with them, and never tired of having them near him. Granddaddy was very special to our sons, Robert and John.

Each time our family went to the states, my parents insisted on us living with them. The first trip to the U.S. our boys had not reached school age, so it was easy to accept their offer. The family traveled together during that year and would return to South Carolina for a week or so after each few weeks on the road.

In the early 1970s, we returned to the states for our second working furlough. That time Mom and Dad had done quite a remodeling job, putting in a second bathroom and a den, so our family could have our own bath and the boys could have a place to play.

The generosity of my parents was a great blessing to us and to our account, cutting the expense of rent stateside. We consider it a privilege to have such concerned parents. During several furloughs, I had at my disposal the family car when Bobby was away. A place to live and a car to drive—what a blessing!

§§

Bobby was reared on a farm forty miles north of Nashville. At times while in the states, our travels kept us in Tennessee for many weeks at a time. Until the death of Mama Poole, the old home place had open doors for us. Bobby's dad died in 1968; therefore, our boys hardly knew him, but they loved and appreciated Mama Poole very much.

During that first trek in the states, with services in the Nashville area, Darrell and Sarah Fulton offered us their home for the weekend while their family went to Mississippi. Our family relaxed after the Fulton family left. Then all of a sudden, a pain started in my right lower abdomen. I had been bothered with a pain in that area at various times during the previous weeks, but this time it was stronger than the previous pain. Nothing I did gave any relief, so about 10:00 P.M. Bobby called his sister requesting that she keep the boys while he took me to the hospital. After exams and tests, the diagnosis was that I had an acute case of appendicitis; therefore, I was admitted to the hospital and surgery was set for early the next morning.

It was a blessing to be in the home of friends, and to have a sister in the same town who willingly took care of the boys. That emergency surgery could have taken place far away from anything familiar, but it happened in home territory, which made things a whole lot easier.

In order to leave the hospital, Bobby paid the partial bill. At that time, they advised him that he would receive the rest of the bill by mail. To our surprise, we never got the rest of the bill, but instead, a letter from Baptist Hospital saying that since we were missionaries the hospital was absorbing the rest. What a blessing!

During the first furlough, Bobby and I spent much of our time on the road, traveling about forty thousand miles and visiting approximately one hundred and twenty churches. Precious people came into our lives who have been prayer and financial supporters through our many years of missionary experience.

One couple in Missouri had our family in their home while we had services in the area. One day the couple had to go into Springfield for a doctor's appointment. When they returned it was late. They had a dairy farm, which meant there were cows to milk. We heard the head of the household tell his wife, "I do not know which is best, to start milking the cows before we go to church or to wait and milk them after the service." There was never any question about not going to church. This type of testimony was such a blessing!

Several years later, that same couple came up to Bobby and me at the National Association. During our conversation, they told us that Robert had left a small toy at their house. They had put it on top of their television set, where it stayed through all those years. They used the toy as a reminder to pray for the Poole family. Thank God for toys left behind.

In Missouri, our family traveled to Pastor Cliff Bowman's house in Liberal. We arrived an hour later than we planned because we had come from an area that did not observe daylight savings time, and that part of Missouri did. We thought the service was to be in Liberal, but it was about 50 miles away. Just ten days earlier I had had an appendectomy, so I was very tired. As quickly as we could, we left for the service.

The Bowmans and our family arrived back in Liberal about the same time, since both families had had services some distance away. This brother was preaching in a revival meeting about 70 miles away. The next day he had to leave before Bobby and I did, so as any good Brazilian would do, Bobby walked out to the car with him. He noticed that the back tires on Bro. Bowman's car were slick. We went on to our different services and then arrived back at the pastor's house for a time of fellowship and a night of rest for our weary bodies.

Bobby could not get those slick tires off his mind, so when the opportunity came he asked this brother what kind of tires he used on his car. He said, "Sears' seconds." The next question was, "How much do they cost?" Then Bobby wrote out a check for the pastor to go to Sears and get two new tires. It was a blessing to be able to help a fellow brother out in time of need.

A month or so later our family was in the state of Oklahoma. The tires on our car were getting a little too thin to travel, as heavily loaded as we were traveling. Bobby felt like he should change them. We were guests in Bob Ketchum's home, so Bobby asked him about the best place to buy tires. He told Bobby that he would take the car the next day and get the tires at the company he and his dad used. When Bobby tried to settle his account, Bob Ketchum told him, "The tires are a gift from my daddy and me." Once again, we thought about the goodness of God. We had given a pastor two second-grade tires and, in return, received four first-grade Dayton Thoroughbreds. One thing we were learning was that we could never outgive God. We learned the joy of giving as well. Many times, God returned the gift in a greater and unexpected way.

§§

After getting back to the field in the early 1970s, one day Bobby came in with a message from the president of a private college located a few blocks from our house. He wanted us to go up to see him. Neither of us had any idea what he wanted, but felt we should go. A couple of days later Bobby and I went up to the college.

He cordially invited us into his office. He soon stated the purpose of the meeting. He wanted to put me on the faculty in the language department. His specific desire was for me to give phonics classes to the students who were studying to become English teachers. Upon his insistence, I accepted the challenge and became a part of the teaching staff. That first year I gave a special course on Saturdays. The next year the school added phonics to the curriculum.

I used this as an opportunity to reach out to as many of those young people as I could. Since we lived near the school, often when students had a break they would come down to our home for a chat in English. In that way, several people came to accept Christ, began attending church, and have been faithful to the Lord all these years.

I definitely did not become a college professor for the financial benefits, but it did help with the construction of the church building. We put the extra income into the work.

§§

One semester I was asked to add English literature to my teaching responsibilities. In my instructions, at the beginning of the semester, I emphatically stressed that each student was to do his own work and no copying on tests or homework was acceptable. I warned them as well that the grade would be "0" for anyone who participated in the wrong act of copying, and a great reduction in grade for the one who allowed someone to copy his paper. My little lecture did not stop there. I spoke to them about the dishonesty of such an act and how, in reality, they were cheating themselves. They needed to study hard to become good teachers.

Everything went fine for a while. I already knew those who were mastering the studies and those who were doing poorly. About a month before the end of the semester, I received their book reports. In grading these papers, I found two exactly alike. Naturally, I had to keep my word. The one who copied got "0" for his grade. The other who allowed the copying of her paper had her grade reduced to "50." The person who received the "0" did not react, but the person who received the "50" showed her disgust, but said nothing.

The semester finally ended with the final exam. When the student who had allowed the copying turned in her paper she said, "Thanks, Mrs. Poole. I did not like the punishment you gave me at first, but now I see how wrong it was. I appreciate you teaching me this valuable lesson."

I silently thanked God for the lesson of honesty learned, and I asked God to drive the point home in the lives of all the students.

After returning to Brazil in 1967, Bobby began checking on land with the hopes of purchasing it so the church could build. He saw a newspaper advertisement about four lots for sale just three blocks from where we lived at the time. He went to get information about the property. The price for the four lots was beyond what he felt the church could manage to pay. In fact, the land fund had just enough to buy one lot, but one lot would never do. The church, with cash in hand for one lot, made the deal to purchase two lots paying the rest in 90 days. Humanly speaking, that was impossible; but with God, it was not. The church paid off the lots within the stipulated time. Their faith had been tested and proven.

The purchasing of the land showed the small group of church members (about 35) what they could do, so enthusiasm to build was high. The church had plans drawn up and approved by the city. As money came in, we purchased materials. Actually, we constructed the building in stages. After we put down the foundation, we collected enough money to put up the walls and cover the building; thus, we resumed construction. After that there was no stopping. People gave and gave, resulting in a completed first floor in 1970, with space for six Sunday school classes and a meeting hall, which would seat one hundred thirty, all paid for by church people of which the missionaries were a part.

◈◈

It was a happy day for the small congregation as they met to dedicate the new building. During the weeks before the dedication, it kept going over in my mind, *I wonder if Bobby will take our piano up to the church for the dedication. It would be nice to have music for the service.* When I made that suggestion to Bobby, he said, "We will take it if you want to, but it will be a gift to the church." Well that was not what I had in mind. I had to pray much about it before I was exactly willing to part with our piano that we had saved years to be able to purchase; but God impressed me to do so.

Not long after that, a missionary friend, Bill Hulett, told us about an American made piano in São Paulo that was for sell, by a missionary couple who was returning to the states to stay. He insisted we go with him to see the piano. The small studio type Wurlitzer had a good sound and was in excellent condition. We paid fifty dollars down with an agreement to pay the rest when we picked up the piano.

Bro. Hulett had already told us that he would lend us the money interest free, with the condition that we pay it back whenever we could. He was aware of the gift of the other piano. So the deal was completed, and we brought the piano to our house in Ribeirão Preto.

Bobby and I went on to the states for our stateside assignment. It had never happened before and has never happened since, but during the first weeks we were in the states, people not knowing the situation were impressed to give us personal money gifts and enough came in to liquidate the piano debt. God is so good! It was wonderful to see God's approval on the gift made to the church. It was great to have the satisfaction of seeing that our boys studied music as well.

One day Robert was in a Sunday school class at Shady Grove Church in Tennessee. The teacher asked if any child wanted to tell how God had supplied a need. He told the class about the piano. He said, "We gave our piano to the church and God gave us another one." The teacher asked, "How?" He really did not know how so he lifted his hands in the air and said, "Just like that!" Later the teacher asked me for the explanation.

§§

Our second furlough time was coming up. We wanted the church to hire a Brazilian young man to be the pastor while we were away, with the idea in mind that if he did well he would become the permanent pastor. Since Dirceu had just graduated from our Brazilian Free Will Baptist Bible College, we invited him to live in our home until we left for furlough.

One problem involved in hiring Dirceu was, the church still owed several thousand dollars that Bobby had borrowed using his credit card. He told the church he would assume that debt. A little surprised and yet not surprised, I asked, "Bobby how can we pay such a large amount when that is just about what we will make while in the U.S.?"

Once again, God supplied. Several people suggested and my sister encouraged me to apply for a teaching position since I would have to stay in one place with our boys to attend school. I made application in two school districts and both of them called me. God was supplying so we could pay the debt for the church. In fact, God supplied enough to cover the debt with some left over!

Before we returned to Brazil, the church was debt free, which made it possible to think of the next phase, the second floor. The same way God again used the people, He again supplied through them, and in 1974 we completed the second floor. That provided space for a library, three more Sunday school rooms, two offices, and a fellowship hall.

§§

Bobby and I, along with Cecilia, made a trip across the city to the land already staked off for the foundation. We could not stop praising the Lord for the works of His hands. Looking at that land, our thoughts went back to the time when we had only hope, confidence, and faith to begin a work there in the suburb of Ipiranga.

It all started when Cecilia, who worked at a day-care center, began telling the stories from the pages of the "wordless book," teaching catchy tunes about Jesus and speaking about His love for them. The little hearts of the children, who were hungry for spiritual food, always wanted to hear another story and to know more of Jesus.

During that time, First Free Will Baptist Church in Ribeirão Preto entered the Fall Enlargement Sunday School Campaign. The idea came to Cecilia to take the children from Ipiranga across town to participate in Sunday school to help them learn more about Jesus. Bro. Antonio and Pastor Bobby put the use of their cars at her disposal and for four Sundays overloaded their vehicles and transported the children. They loved the ride, but were also happy for the opportunity to be in Sunday school.

The contest passed without the church being a winner, but a door had opened to begin a work on the other side of town. Bobby and I felt that God wanted a work in that area of the city. There were the questions of how and where.

Cecilia tried to get permission to use the school where she taught, but that did not work out. We started our search for a house. Soon we found a vacant house. Even though it was very old, our hearts were happy because it appeared to be the right place. Bobby approached the owner and talked to him about renting the house. It was not for rent, only for sale.

Even that did not discourage the three who were diligently searching. We held our first Bible lesson sitting on the grass beneath the bright, hot sun. For the next meeting the shade of a tree was a welcomed place. For a number a weeks, we held Sunday school in the shade of that tree. Even in all of that, the Lord was blessing!

A house, which they called a church, was located and rented. The owner was unable to finish building it, so the First Free Will Baptist Church took on the project of getting it into a usable state. We moved the afternoon Sunday school from underneath the tree to the little church building. Soon a Wednesday night service, directed by Bro. Antonio, became a reality.

The people of the First Free Will Baptist Church became involved in the new work. As the people prayed for the new venture, some of them felt the Lord leading them to cooperate with the teaching responsibilities at the new church.

During the first year, we had our first vacation Bible school. Overflowing crowds, with an average attendance of 87 children, young people, and adults, encouraged those working with the church. One worker said, "Each time we go to Iprianga, we feel that it is 'the place' God has chosen. We are thankful to the Lord that we are being used as His instruments."

Soon it was evident that we needed to build a more adequate meeting place with an auditorium for services. Some months later the Lord, who does not forsake those who really believe in Him, gave us a desire to help obtain a place of worship. We started searching for land. There were plenty of lots available; but none of them seemed to be the right place. Then one day it was brought to our memory that Grandmother Isabel at one time had land in the immediate area. When she purchased it, she had a desire that it would be used for a church someday. It would be ideal since it was not one, but four lots. But her lawyer son had purchased the land from her to help meet her financial needs.

Bobby felt impressed that he should call Dr. Nereu, so he did. He called to find out about the possibility of obtaining the land for the church and, if so, what the price would be. Dr. Nereu said that he would be going to Ribeirão Preto the next week, and he would talk it over with his wife and they would give him an answer while in Ribeirão Preto. Just before hanging up the phone Bobby told Dr. Nereu, "You know how small churches are. We ask you to give us the very best price possible."

Five days later, Dr. Nereu called and asked Bobby to meet him at his mother's house. With the formal greetings over, the subject of the land came up. Dr. Nereu and his wife Geninha told the story of how they had needed money when constructing their house so she had come to Ribeirão Preto to put the property on the market. Unable to sell it, they finally took it off the market. Dr. Nereu also said they felt God had saved it for a purpose. Considering all these factors, they had decided to give the very best price possible. All the church needed to pay was cost of the transfer of the deed into the name of the church. Bobby was without words, but not without tears—and a rejoicing heart.

Time was running out to get a building up before our third furlough. The First Church decided to put up a meeting hall, which included two Sunday school rooms and two rest rooms. During the last six weeks before we left for the U.S. for stateside assignment, our task was to see that building become a reality. A bricklayer by trade, a deacon in the First Free Will Baptist Church donated his time to build the building.

Not only was time running out, but also money had come to an abrupt end. Bills had to be paid. Bobby used a motorcycle for transportation because gasoline was almost five dollars a gallon. He wanted to have some money to put down on a car when we got to the states, so he sold his motorcycle. One day he came in and said, "I used the motorcycle money to pay construction bills today." I quickly responded, "What are we going to do? Now we don't have a down payment for a car." Bobby simply answered, "God will supply."

The last Saturday night before leaving for the states on Monday, Bobby and I, along with the people of the first church, dedicated the new building in Ipiranga to the glory of His grace. The Lord had done great things through the people of the First Free Will Baptist Church!

Our family flew into Florence, South Carolina for stateside assignment. Naturally, a large group of people were at the airport to greet us. We noticed that the people were anxious for us to get our luggage and move on out to the parking lot.

When we got out into the parking lot, they loaded our luggage into a nice looking, green and cream Ford. It was one of the top models. Then a friend of many years stepped up and said, "Bobby and Geneva, come over here." Naturally, we obeyed. He took two sets of keys from his pocket, held them up, and said, "This is your car to use this year. The insurance is already paid. Trust it will be a blessing to you. Use it, then return it when you are finished with your year of stateside assignment."

Blessing! It was already a blessing, just knowing how God works when we are willing to give to Him! He had already given us so much more than we thought imaginable.

※

Training workers for the harvest fields has been our focus since the very beginning. At first, I trained our Sunday school teachers on a one-to-one basis. During those first years, I would invite a person who had the desire and possibilities of becoming a teacher to my Sunday school class. Each Sunday I gave the prospective teacher a responsibility with training sessions as well, thus gradually turning the class over to her until she gave a couple of complete lessons. Then the class divided, and we started a new class. That process continued until we had teachers for all of the Sunday school classes.

A new door opened to us in 1973, eleven years after the beginning of the work in Ribeirão Preto. Near the end of 1972, four young people were talking with Bobby and me about going to Word of Life Bible College. Bobby knew that, if they went, they would not likely return to Free Will Baptists and their doctrine would be changed, especially in the area of eternal security. Out of the clear blue, Bobby asked the four students that if a Bible Institute opened in the church, would they stay and study in Ribeirão Preto. All four of them answered yes. Thus, a new door opened when, with four students, the Bible Institute was born. We consider it one of the most important decisions made in our work.

Soon the Bible Institute became a Bible College, offering a Bachelor of Arts degree in Bible and theology. Cecilia Virdes, the first graduate, left in 1980 for her missionary assignment in the territory of Roraima, an area in the northern most part of Brazil. For a number of years she worked under MEVA, the Brazilian Branch of Unevangelized Fields Mission, but received her support from Free Will Baptists in Brazil. Her mission vision has helped to widen the mission vision of the whole church.

The Free Will Baptist Church in Ribeirão Preto changed tremendously as Sunday school teachers, laymen, and deacons sacrificed their time to study the Word through the local Bible College classes. No other one thing has done so much for the church.

The church and college, which had humble beginnings, have been able to reach out to doctors, lawyers, teachers, university professors, economists, storeowners, and the simplest gardener.

The young people were active in evangelism. César was the instrument God used to bring a number of young people to the Lord.

One day Bobby saw César walking some distance in front of him, just about the time César passed a car where a passenger was waiting. He pulled out a tract, exchanged a few words with the person, gave him the tract and went on his way. Bobby noticed that the person who received the tract threw it out the window. By that time, Bobby was near the car. He picked up the tract and politely said, "I think you dropped this" and returned the tract to the person. He went on his way into the post office. When he came out, he noticed that the person was reading the tract. The printed word can have an influence upon people.

One day Bobby and I were at the clinic hospital to make a visit. As we entered the elevator, we gave the operator the number of the floor. As soon as we started climbing Bobby said, "Your last trip, will it be up or down?" She thought a few seconds and then exclaimed, "I hope it will be up." That opened the door to tell her quickly how she could be sure. We talked until she received a signal to go to another floor.

We should use every means for the furtherance of the gospel. In 1980 a new ministry came into being—a telephone ministry. Often through the call-back number Bobby and I have been able to help that lost one find Jesus, that troubled one find peace, that desperate one grasp hope, or that blind one see the light. Because of the telephone ministry, counseling has become a vital part of the church's ministries.

Around the same time, a home Bible-study ministry had its beginning, using the "Source of Light" materials. Hundreds of students as near as next door to the church and as far as Mozambique in Africa have taken the course. At one time there were as many as 700 enrolled; thus, the course was an instrument helping people study the Word of God. Many testimonies came of people accepting the Lord. They were encouraged to find an evangelical church to attend and through that church serve the Lord.

At about the same time, Bobby and I wrote the following in our newsletter: "Since we have around one hundred in Sunday school and in the night services; since we have the responsibilities of two other churches—Ipiranga and Jaboticabal, which at the moment is without a pastor; since we see a renewed desire among the people to study in the Bible College; since we need to build a larger building; since we see a greater interest in missions; since we have a larger group of prayer warriors; and since we have observed in the believers a greater knowledge of God's Word, we have a feeling greater things are going to be accomplished in Ribeirão Preto for Christ's glory."

※

From a stack of newsletters, I quickly read one. I will share it with you to help you see the type of schedule we were keeping at that time.

March 20, 1975

Dear Friends,

Rest and relaxation were what the Pooles needed. To get this we rented a small apartment on the oceanfront. Early mornings and late afternoons, everyone took a dip in the ocean. The rest of the day, we spent playing games, boating, riding along the ocean highway, reading, etc. Twice we visited a local Baptist church. It was a wonderful few days, but we became anxious to get back into the work!

The day after arriving home, Bobby had a workshop with the pastors in the São Paulo area. Of course, the meal for fourteen was my responsibility. They felt the direction of the Holy Spirit during the whole meeting. Studies given were of interest and instructive.

Busy days lay ahead. The Bible Institute is to begin with a dinner on the following Friday night and classes on Monday night. The house hummed busily with preparations—both for the supper and the classes as well. (Classes began with eight students.)

That same weekend we had in our home Mr. Perry Temple, the Executive Secretary of Bible Literature International. His interest is better literature for mission work. The Lord used him to be a blessing to us.

By March, classes in two schools, both Portuguese and English, along with swimming and music had already started for the boys, which kept everyone on a time chart. The boys are doing just fine. Keeping them busy has not stunted their growth at all. Robert, the twelve-year-old, weighs one hundred and twenty pounds and is five feet and seven inches tall. John is somewhat smaller for his age.

An extracurricular activity for the first week in March was a supper sponsored by the young married couples Sunday school class. Out of the forty-six present, there were sixteen unchurched. The Holy Spirit led during the whole evening, even in the games played. The program closed out with an interesting devotional talk, illustrating on the blackboard the plan of salvation. As a result, there were tears, many comments about spiritual needs, and invitations for visits or Bible studies in homes. Already one couple has joined the Sunday school class. We are praying that through these contacts, in the near future we are going to see a number of couples accepting Christ and serving Him. Pray with us for these dear people.

Work has begun on the church building again. Cash on hand is only a fraction of the amount needed, but the people are enthusiastic about putting up the second floor. This enthusiasm is going to help in raising the necessary funds.

Good Friday is the day of the annual fellowship meeting of the Free Will Baptists in the state of São Paulo. The host church, Ribeirão Preto, is expecting about two hundred and fifty to attend. We trust the Lord will give a great day! [Around three hundred attended.]

An attendance campaign, 'Double the Enrollment,' has been set for April, May, and June. To be enrolled a person must come at least three Sundays straight. Pray that the people will accept the challenge to work, and that we will see many saved and begin serving the Lord.

Because of Christ,
Bobby and Geneva

§♂

Some years ago, in fact during our first term on the field, we cried out to the Lord about the need for someone with music ability. That cry came in desperation because we knew good music is not only a way of worshiping God, but also a way of attracting people who love music to the church, where they can learn about Christ through the preaching of the Word. Before long an answer came. A widowed missionary living in town began playing for our services, using a little portable electric organ donated by a World Gospel Crusades couple. After she left, God supplied another person and another person to play that little organ.

On June 5, 1983, we were reminded again of God's faithfulness in answering and continuing to answer prayer. The music department of First Free Will Baptist Church sponsored an hour and a half musical program called "Night of Praise," which was presented by forty people. Of those forty, nineteen played instruments. The night was truly a night of praise.

Bobby and I wrote about the event, "We are grateful that there are at least seventeen in the church who play the piano and eight or more who play the guitar. Has not God graciously answered our plea for His help? The wonderful thing about this is that these are people who are dedicated to the Lord and His work and desire to be used for the glory of His grace."

06.
TESTIMONIES THROUGH THE YEARS

"This is the disciple which testifieth of these things, and wrote these things: and we know that his testimony is true." JOHN 21:24

Nothing is more convincing than the life and the daily walk of a person for others to know he has truly accepted Christ as his personal Savior. Emilia dos Santos was one of the first people we won to the Lord in Ribeirao Preto. She was a very simple, but intelligent woman. The following is her testimony.

"Last year was the turning point in my life." These words were spoken to me by that faithful Christian woman. She was the mother of eight living children at the time. All of her married life she had struggled to keep food and clothing for herself and her children.

She said her hatred for her husband began some years earlier when there was only one child. Her husband was unfaithful to her. At that time, no woman would think of leaving her husband—no matter what he did. In fact, a husband's unfaithfulness was almost expected because of the Brazilian mindset. She was left at home most of the time while he spent a big part of his earnings and evenings drinking and having a good time at dances and movies. Because of the situation, Emilia was forced to work outside the home.

Emilia felt that her husband's unfaithfulness gave her the liberty to date, but has always been thankful that she never did. Her life was sad and empty. Trying to fill the emptiness with pleasures of the world was only in vain. Dancing and movies only left her body physically tired for the next day's work and gave her no peace within.

The hatred for her husband increased until she had a constant desire to kill him. That desire remained with her for years. One night she told me her testimony, "Dona Geni [Mrs. Geneva], it was not until I started attending the Free Will Baptist church, accepted Christ as my personal Savior, and surrendered my life, my family, and my problems to God that I found peace and the hatred left me. Now I am praying that my husband will also come to know Christ."

Since the mother became a Christian, she and her eight children are in Sunday school and church services. Her husband has gone to church only a few times. Most of her children have accepted the Lord and have continued to serve Him.

Another interesting fact about Dona Emilia is that when she became a Christian she did not know how to read, but several of her children did. She learned to read with the help of her children using the Bible as her textbook.

༺༻

The "god" of many Brazilian youth is a little round monster called "Futebol" (soccer ball). They talk it, eat it, sleep it, dream it, and, of course, play it every minute they have to spare. For Benedito it was no different. He loved soccer!

Benedito or Dito as he was called, began attending the Free Will Baptist congregation in Ribeirão Preto after his mother became a Christian. He attended faithfully for a year but did not make a decision for Christ. His "god" stood between him and a personal commitment of his life to Christ.

At that time Dito became a "regular" on the team who visited Albertina, a nearby farm village. It was on one of those trips during the visit of General Director Reford Wilson that Dito came to the foot of the cross. Perhaps his story can best be told in the words of Bro. Wilson: "On the way out of town, going to the farm service, we passed a soccer stadium. Dito began telling me about some of the players and fantastic sums of money they were paid. I looked at Benedito and asked him a Holy Spirit directed question, 'Benedito, what do you want out of life?'"

"I had expected him to answer that his desire was to have a machine shop of his own or to become a famous soccer player. God's Spirit, however, directed his answer. He said, 'I want salvation most of all.'"

Bobby asked, 'Benedito, do you mean you want to be saved now?' Without hesitation he replied, "I do." Bobby pulled the jeep to the side of the rough, dirt road where we prayed with Benedito and he accepted Christ as his Savior. We went on our way rejoicing."

Since Sunday is the day to play soccer in Brazil, it was not easy for Dito not to let his desire for soccer to control him. It was a battle, but God was faithful. His mother said a few weeks later that he had sold his cleats and other soccer equipment.

On February 26, 1964, Bobby and I wrote, "Our visitation brings us in contact with many heart touching situations." I would like to relate the following experience:

Our visits one Saturday afternoon took us into a home where the grandfather was very sick. It was evident that his time on earth would be short, so in the few minutes available we gave the gospel message to the aged man and his family. Within a few days, the man had gone on to meet his Maker; nevertheless, God used his death to open the hearts of members of his family. Within a short time after that initial contact, at least fifteen people had made decisions to follow Christ.

One of these was Olimpia, his widow, in her mid-seventies who had never learned to read or write. She was not satisfied with her life; she wanted a Savior. She accepted Christ and, even though she was almost blind physically, her eyes were opened spiritually. Her simple faith helped her to find a true friend in Jesus.

BenVinda, mother of five and daughter of Olimpia, was the first to accept Christ after the death of her father. Sometime earlier the father of her five children had died. She revealed a problem common to Brazil: she was not married to the man she was living with. After she and Sabastião accepted Christ as their Savior, they realized they needed to do something about their marital situation. After a time of intensive battle within their hearts, they chose to go their separate ways. Their simple faith carried them through the separation.

Marianete, BenVinda's daughter, started attending Sunday school and through the teaching of the Word accepted Christ. Although working as a maid and studying at night, she continued faithful. She was a happy, smiling girl who showed forth the love of Christ through her daily walk with Him.

Luzianete, also Benvinda's daughter, was living with her husband and small children in the state of Goiás, but because of drought moved to Ribeirão Preto to find a job. In Goiás she had attended a Pentecostal church, but when she came to the Free Will Baptist Church, she made a commitment to give her life to Christ and became a happy Christian.

❦

Ercília, the wife of a taxi driver was faithful in the Catholic Church. She was employed in cleaning services for the largest Catholic Church in town, yet there was no peace in her heart. Quite often, she went to the movies trying to fill her empty life.

One day after work, she arrived at her small home and found a gospel tract on the ground. On the cover were the words, "God Calls." She commented later, "Those words never left me, and it was then I began to search for the truth."

Shortly afterwards Jehovah Witness tried to get her involved with their studies, but she could not accept their doctrine. That gave her a greater desire to know the truth.

In the early part of 1960, her family moved to Ribeirão Preto. One day while speaking with a relative about her desire to know the truth, the relative was impressed to give her a Bible and that gave her an opportunity to study the Word.

Dona Ercília began working as a cook at a boarding house. One night while she was washing dishes, she heard in the distance the words of a hymn: "Let the light of heaven enter. Open wide the door of your heart and let the light of heaven enter." She left her dishes and went in search of the music. It was a group at the Adventist Church nearby. Standing near the door, she had an urge to enter, so she did. For a while, she attended that church.

Later she decided that she could not follow the doctrine of the Adventist Church. In August of 1963, she came to a service at the Free Will Baptist church. Soon she was faithful, made a decision to follow Christ as her Lord and Savior, and then followed the Lord in baptism. She testifies, "Now I have found the truth. I want to learn more about Christ my Savior and bring others to Him."

§§

Delermando was perhaps the first Free Will Baptist convert in Brazil. He made his decision to follow Christ during a message preached by senior missionary Thomas H. Willey on his survey trip of Brazil. He was a lad of eighteen and, soon after his conversion he was given the opportunity to preach in the street services.

Feeling the need for preparation, Delermando went to a Bible Institute in another state for a year and a half. Upon his return to Campinas, he entered the Free Will Baptist institute, which had just begun there and studied for another year. Then he was called upon by his country to serve a year in the armed services.

Completing his army duties, Delermando moved to Ribeirão Preto to work with the congregation started there. Soon he became involved in the work doing many of the things necessary to get a new work going—preaching, teaching, visiting, and distributing tracts—and he worked part-time selling books to help supplement his income.

Delermando was a great help to the work, but after a time he began doing things that were not a good testimony, such as preaching on tithing and then not tithing. In their mentoring times, Bobby approached him about it and other aspects of his ministry as well. After a time no changes were made. The next time Bobby approached Delermando, Bobby told him about the seriousness of being a hypocrite. He said to Dilermando,

"God's hand is upon you in the ministry, and God's hand can be upon you to get you out of the ministry."

Within a short time, Delermando caught a very bad cold, which lingered and turned into tuberculosis. Within a year, he was taken on to heaven. You be the judge if that was just circumstances or the hand of God working.

※

Rosalina was not perfect. She had her problems in her Christian walk, but she remained faithful even after disciplinary action by the church.

About daybreak one morning, Rosalina appeared at our home. She gave her plight. Her mother had had a stroke and she did not want her to die. She gave her request with such fervor that we led the church to ask God to spare her mother's life. God gave that Christian her desire, but also sent her leanness of soul. For nine long years, her mother was bedridden. Rosalina had full responsibility to care for her. The sad part of the story is that, even after her mother's death, Rosalina never got back in church.

God taught us a valuable lesson. It definitely is best to ask God that His will be done. The case of Rosalina brought Psalm 106:15 to our minds: "And he gave them their request; but sent leanness into their soul." We did not want to witness other cases like this one.

※

The words were hand lettered on the glass plaque we found at our house after returning from the annual Field Council Meeting of Free Will Baptist missionaries. "Then spoke Jesus again unto them, saying, I am the light of the world, he that followeth me shall not walk in darkness, but shall have the light of life." A message had been left with the plaque saying that the maker would return to see if he had left it at the right place.

It is necessary to go back about a year and a half to bring you up to date on the story. Bobby and Manoel, a blind boy who played the accordion, were holding weekly services in a jail that housed about seventy-five inmates. At times as many as thirty-five prisoners attended the services. A number of them received gospel literature, and some were taking the "Luz de Vida" (Light of Life) study course on the Book of John.

Belchior enrolled in that course. Shortly after the completion of the course, he was transferred to a prison and all contact with him was lost—that is, until much later.

Freed from prison, he immediately set out to find the one who had given him the study course. He had the church address stamped on the back of his study course booklet, so he sought out the church only to find no one present. A woman he met on the sidewalk nearby gave him the name of the street where the pastor resided. Following directions, he found Yara Street, a street only three blocks long, chose a house to seek further information. To his surprise, it was our house, but only the girl who helped me was there.

Belchior made the plaque while in prison. He left it with a promise to return. Sunday morning he came to the church for Sunday school. Bobby immediately recognized him and indeed was happy to see him.

Belchior gave us a little of his history—not boastfully but very humbly. He had a Catholic background with his mother leaning toward Spiritism. After the death of his father, he came to a state of financial desperation. Needing money and taking bad advice from so-called friends, he began buying stolen articles and reselling them. He said he actually did a little stealing, but tried to live an honest life. When the gang was caught, he landed in prison for about four years.

He told us, "Thirty prisoners have already been or soon will be given their freedom. I fear that out of the thirty only one will not return to prison in the near future. After I have prepared myself I am going to return to tell them about Christ."

The first term, a five-year one, was quickly ending. We were preparing for the trip back to our home country. Emotions were running high! Happiness dominated when thinking of returning to the U.S.; however, on the other hand, sadness lingered as we thought of the believers we were leaving behind. The church people and our friends were sad as well.

Let me share with you the minutes of the going away meeting.

"On the fourth of December, 1965, a meeting was held in the residence of Isabel de Melo. It was a meeting to give thanks for the blessings of God, which the members of the Free Will Baptist Church in Ribeirão Preto had received since its beginning four years earlier. Practically all the church people and six visitors were present.

Missionary Eula Mae Martin opened the meeting by commenting on the way Jesus had done great things; therefore, for that reason we were happy. Everyone sang the chorus, *I am Happy* and *I Have Decided to Follow Jesus*, and the hymn, *Holy, Holy, Holy*, with much enthusiasm.

Maria from Jataí, Goiás read Psalm 103. Afterwards Dona Isabel shared some thoughts about the psalm, pointing out the importance of reading and meditating upon the Bible for spiritual food.

Next Maria dos Santos gave her testimony about the blessings she had received during her time of studies in the Bible Institute in Jaboticabal. Then Rosalina gave her testimony, 'The date of December 23, 1964, I will never forget because it is the date of my conversion during a visit by Pastor Bobby. In a marvelous way, I stopped smoking. I followed the Lord in baptism in January of 1965. I became a new creature in Christ; today I am on fire with a love for Christ. I am so thankful that my family also has accepted Christ. To be different is not difficult when Christ is working in the heart.'

Benedita gave her testimony of the transformation since she had Christ living in her heart. She began to cry because the Poole family would soon be leaving to return to the United States. She was also sad because Maria das Graças, her daughter, was not present because she was in the hospital.

Geralda gave her testimony saying that she had left a life of sin, which included the habit of smoking. Since her conversion she is trusting God. Emília gave her testimony that knowing Christ has made a difference in her life. Her nine children are also in the way of the Lord. She was so thankful that her two oldest children were studying the Bible at the Free Will Baptist Bible Institute in Jaboticabal. Those two were present and commented on passages of Scripture. Maria used John 3:16 and Ezekiel 18:30–32 and Benedito spoke on Psalm 89. Conceição gave her testimony saying that, after she accepted Christ as her personal Savior, her oldest son did not make her cry anymore. That shows that the power of prayer will transform. She was very happy because she was to be baptized the next day. João Jacinto, a young person faithful to the Lord, spoke a few words as well.

The chorus, *I feel It in My Heart* was sung.

Dona Isabel showed the tablecloth that she had embroidered (using her regular sewing machine) for the land fund campaign. She asked each family to buy a square in which to embroider their names. All money raised would go to the land fund. (Even after 45 years I still have that tablecloth.)

Following that, Pastor Bobby, Dona Geni and their two sons, Robert, and John received presents. Dr. Alan Gordon, his wife, and children received small gifts as well.

After the hymn *God Be With You,* Pastor Bobby offered up to the Lord a prayer of thanksgiving.

The meeting closed with not only a time of fellowship with refreshments, but also happiness and peace.

Ribeirão Preto, the 5th of December of 1965"

"The greatest day of my life was when I entered the Free Will Baptist Church, heard the gospel and accepted Jesus Christ as my Savior," were the words of Manuel Lourenço who was born in the north of Brazil in 1943. Leaving home at the age of ten, he began a search for treatment for his eyes. His wanderings took him into many places, but he never found the care he was looking for, and his eyes steadily became dimmer. By the age of sixteen, he lost his sight completely. Somehow he found his way to the city of Ribeirão Preto where he lived in a home for the blind.

One of the women from the Free Will Baptist church contacted the home about a Christmas meeting. Because of that meeting Manuel, along with several others, began attending the services and soon he accepted Christ as Savior. Manuel was a blessing to the work of the Lord. He played the accordion, which helped with the music in the church, in Albertina, and for the services in the jail. It was a joy to work together with that servant of God. It was indeed a blessing to see him use his Bible in Braille to give forth God's Word! Bobby was able to obtain Bible portions in Braille in Portuguese from a U.S. mission group that ministered to the blind. Those Bible portions were a great help and blessing to Manuel.

There was a time when Bobby and I, after evaluating our outreach, decided that we must reach couples. Instead of going as much from house to house during the day when only the wife was at home, we started making visits by appointments. In that way, we were able to talk with both the husband and wife.

Domingos, a church member, set up one of these appointments. In fact, for that first visit into the home of Marçal and Erminia, Domingos went with us. They allowed us to make the visit because they needed help. Strange things were happening around the house. Since we were missionaries, it might help to have us pray over the house.

That night turned out to be a blessing. Both of them made decisions to follow the Lord Jesus. Marçal came to church for almost every service after that decision and began to grow spiritually. Erminia had some things in her life that she did not want to give up, so she was always thwarted in her Christian walk. For years and years now, Marçal has been a deacon in the First Free Will Baptist Church. (In 2009, after Erminia lay in a coma in the hospital for several months, she went on to meet the Lord.)

What Marçal had received he wanted to share with others. He began talking to various members of his family and to people at the supermarket where he was a manager. That did not go well with a few people, so one complained to the owner, Marçal's brother-in-law. That resulted in Marçal losing his job. But he stayed faithful to his Savior and Lord, thus God supplied him with a better job as manager of a much larger supermarket.

During his long life Marçal's father-in-law, Sr. Miguel, had experienced Catholicism, spiritism, Jehovah's Witness, and many other "isms", but never found peace. He listened as Marçal told him about his newfound faith. When Sr. Miguel was in his early nineties, he went to live in the home of Marçal and Erminia, at which time he began attending church. Soon he made his decision to follow Christ and could not stop talking about his newfound faith. In fact, he would go to his son's supermarket (the one where Marçal lost his job), talk about his Lord, and give out tracts to people who entered the store. Each Sunday he would almost empty the tract rack, filling his pockets with tracts to give out before he returned to church. What an example to all of us was that man of God! Sr. Miquel was saved at age ninety-one and died at ninety-six. Thus, he had a short time to do what he did for the Lord. During that period, he was faithful in service.

Cold chills swept over Bobby and me from head to toe as we entered the door. Realizing we were entering Satan's territory, silently we cried out to God for protection and wisdom.

No, we were not entering a spiritist center, but had simply gone to call on one of the new Christians whose family was involved in spiritism.

That visit in particular we will never be able to forget. One of the male family members was full of jeering remarks about religion. Sometimes he spoke with such scornful derision that it was almost unbearable for his sister who had just found life in Christ. The mother wanted to be nice, but not to the point of hearing anything that would thrust any light on her evil ways. Neither was she concerned about her daughter, since religion was just another one of her wild ideas that would blow over shortly.

As we left that home, all we could do was breathe a silent prayer. How that babe in Christ needed our prayers! "Lord, help her. Give her strength and wisdom," was our silent plea.

A myriad of questions flashed through our minds. *Was that the pressure under which Cecilia had to live? Would she remain true to her newfound faith under those circumstances? Would we be able to help this family come to know Christ?*

Cecilia did not give up, but instead she became more involved in the work of the Lord. As time passed the jeering remarks turned into extreme pressure to make her abandon her faith. That became even more drastic when she was able to get her younger sister to attend church with her.

With a great desire to do God's will, Cecilia entered the Bible institute, but times of sadness often fell upon her. Satanic depression would overcome her to the extent that she would cry, and classes could not continue until after resisting, in extensive times of prayer.

"Lord, give us your wisdom," was our sincere cry to God. Through hours and hours of counseling and prayer, little by little we were able to see her through to complete victory.

Many times, we told Cecilia, "Do not give up. Trust in God. He will give you victory." In saying that to her, we were also exhorting ourselves to not become discouraged. We kept Galatians 6:9 constantly before us: "And let us not be weary in well doing: for in due season we shall reap, if we faint not."

Victory did come, but not without its price. There were years of conflicts followed by calmness, sufferings followed by blessings, and defeats followed by victories. Finally, a lasting victory was won!

The next big blow did not remove Cecilia's steadfastness.

"To work among the Indians. Only over my dead body," was the mothers wail when she learned that Cecilia had answered God's call for her life.

Much prayer, serious preparation, and enduring patience went together to bring the mother to the acceptance of her daughter living in an Indian village; but it did happen. Cecilia served more than eight years under MEVA (the Brazilian branch of Unevangelized Fields Mission) in the north of Brazil.

§§

Sometimes it is difficult to see a need beyond those of our immediate family and friends, and most often the needs are only pertaining to the physical and material. It is sad to say, but quite often the spiritual needs of others never get into the visible picture; therefore, they are left unheeded.

Perhaps the burdens of the physical and material are the result of not taking care of the spiritual. Mathew 6:33, "But seek ye first the kingdom of God, and his righteousness; and all these things [physical and material] shall be added unto you."

During the time Cecilia was working among the Indians, the Free Will Baptist churches in Brazil supported her. There were nine women who tried to look beyond themselves to help others in need. These women were not rich—just working class—but they desired, most of all, to please their Master by doing what they could for the propagating of the Good News.

Let us begin with Grandmother Isabel, who had just had her eighty-third birthday. Prayer was her tool. She rose early for her prayer time. People gave their urgent requests to her. Prayer is not all she did; she baked and embroidered and gave each month's proceeds to the missions offering. Along with Grandmother Isabel, the other eight women made time to do their cooking, baking, and crafts, so each one could have something to add to the offering.

Berenice gave herself a birthday party. She occupied herself with preparations. She invited her friends, making the request that she receive no gifts for herself, but an offering to be used for missions. With a calm delight, she was able to give in the currency of the day the equivalent of fifty dollars!

It was a surprise to most of the women that their yearly offering totaled over one thousand dollars, an average of about ten dollars per member per month! A few thought that it should have been more. They had gotten off to a slow start and the enthusiasm only took on momentum after the first three months. That was an extraordinary offering in a third world country.

To these women, giving was not the only way of looking beyond. They had a weekly prayer meeting. That was an unusual meeting. There was no Bible study and no singing, just the giving of prayer requests, usually one at a time with few details, and a time of prayer for that request. The meeting began at 8:00 and never ended before 10:00; and quite often the leader had to say, "Ladies, this is good, but we need to go. Let's have other requests to remember at home."

They learned that when they really pray, for instance for the salvation of a friend, then they get involved to win that friend. That prayer meeting led the women not only to look beyond, but also to go beyond.

Who are these women? They are Brazilians who love their Savior. They are from the First Free Will Baptist Church in Ribeirão Preto, S. P., Brazil.

The way they worked in order for others to be able to hear the good news, was evidence that they were truly thankful that someone had come to tell them. Bobby and I have been in Brazil for fifty years because our Free Will Baptist people in the U.S. are looking beyond as well.

§§

There are many disappointments in working with people. Many follow through with the Lord and stay faithful. Cecilia has been used greatly in the work of the Lord, but today, 2009, she is inactive. She has allowed things to come into her life that caused her to be "put on the shelf." We, your missionaries, poured much time, prayer, and sacrifice into that one life which today is no longer active in the work of the Lord. How sad! Oh, how this must break the heart of our Savior!

Let us always remember that our spirituality today is never sufficient for tomorrow. We must renew it daily.

§§

Three children, all junior or adolescent ages, began coming to Sunday school because of the invitation of their cousins who were already attending. They became excited about going to church and soon became a part of the church family. Their mother wanted to know what was causing the excitement, so she started attending with them. Soon the Holy Spirit convicted her of her need of a Savior and she accepted Christ. By that time the dad, a very firm practicing Catholic, was not pleased at all. He did not want his family to become involved with that "false religion." He tried to convince his wife to go with him to the Catholic Church. She had been reared a Catholic, but she did not feel that what she and the children were receiving was wrong. It all came directly from the Word of God.

The participation in the Free Will Baptist Church caused a rift over religion, which was getting larger each day. The mother came to me to ask counsel. Before we made any decision about the way to handle the situation, we asked the church to pray.

The next time the mother and I talked about the problem, the couple still had not agreed upon a solution. The husband and father wanted the priest to decide. My counsel was that he was the head of the household; therefore allow him to do as he desired. The church prayed, knowing that God was in control. The priest, Dom Aparício, was invited to the home of the couple to talk, at which time the situation was put before him. Dom Aparício and Bobby had talked on a number of occasions. With no hesitation, he said, "I know Pastor Bobby. You can trust him to teach God's Word. My suggestion is to allow your family to continue going to that church." That settled the matter; they continued.

"I have heard enough!" was what I wanted to blurt out, but as politely as I could I said good-bye and put the phone back on the hook.

As I sat there stunned, tears began to stream down my already flushed cheeks. All I could pray was, "Lord, help her. Please help her. I do not know how."

Sadness flooded my heart as I thought about the open rebellion. It was difficult to believe that this woman had been one of the most faithful to the Lord and His work. As a young Christian, she had had grown spiritually as she studied the Word.

In my mind, I went back over the happenings of the past few weeks. There was the Sunday when she asked Bobby to help her son, who was breaking a rule of the Bible College where he was studying. I could still see the concern in the mother's eyes.

Bobby, with all the love and help he knew how to give, called the student in and counseled him about the problem. Bobby told him to let God work in his life, and that he would talk with him later about his decision. A reply quickly came, "I already know what I am going to do. I am going to continue smoking." Instead of repenting, he rebelled. Bobby finally told him, "You have the right of choice, but you do not control the outcome." The outcome was his dismissal from school and consequently the school quartet.

Our constant prayer was, "Lord, give us wisdom. Help us to help those who have rebelled."

It soon became evident that the mother had changed her mind and was putting all the blame on Bobby for her son's rebellion. She was showing just as much rebellion as her son.

As time passed, both mother and son dropped out of church. All that Bobby and I could do was pray. It was a sad situation as the days slipped into weeks and the weeks into months, with the rebellion becoming more evident each day. The ex-student came to the church and stayed outside smoking while the people entered and left the services.

The mother struck out to hurt Bobby and me. In a church business meeting, she had asked Bobby to leave the phone that the mission had purchased for our personal use at the church, and use an extra phone which she owned at our house. At that time, a phone line cost about fifteen-hundred dollars. During her rebellion, she wanted to charge rent for her phone. What a stink she caused when Bobby refused to pay rent for the phone she had offered us to use. She removed the phone, making it necessary for us to purchase one.

One thing led to another. One day Bobby and I learned, through the mission office, that the mother had written a letter asking the office to remove us from Brazil.

The church leaders were very much aware of the problem and knew they had to deal with it. A night was set to meet with the mother; however, before she learned of the meeting she called our home phone. I answered the phone. With a voice full of emotion, she quickly asked if Pastor Bobby was in. I was unable to read her emotions, so quickly called Bobby to the phone.

Only hearing a one-sided conversation, I sensed joy for I knew a miracle had happened. The mother had asked to meet with the church board because she had a confession to make.

Tears of joy came into the eyes of the group that night as she told her story. She said that she knew how wrong she had been and that, even though she had stopped going to church, she had not stopped reading the Bible. She explained how she was afraid God would convict her if she read the New Testament, so she read in the Old Testament only. She had gotten into the book of I Samuel when the words from 15:23 jumped from the page and hit her: "Rebellion is as the sin of witchcraft." She said she had already asked forgiveness from the Lord, but wanted to ask the church to forgive her also. She was also willing to make restitution!

God worked and she did everything the church asked her to do to set aright the wrongs done. What a blessing it was to have her back in church and once again serving the Lord!

The miracle did not stop there. Within a few months time the son had repented, had gotten back into church, and was growing spiritually.

It was the year of the twenty-fifth anniversary of the Brazilian church. We had the main celebration in Araras during an association meeting. I wrote the following about that celebration.

"At first glance you could have easily thought you were not in a foreign country as the modern bus pulled up in front of the church. That is until you began to look more closely. The bus was indeed modern, but had not been cleaned after its last trip. The windshield was fairly well spattered with insects, which had met their destiny the night before. The restroom was tightly locked up because it was in dire need of a cleaning.

Impossible! Yes, it is virtually impossible to do things on time in Brazil. The bus was thirty minutes late getting to the church, therefore, thirty minutes late getting to its destination, Araras.

That is how our Good Friday began. Although there were the inconveniences that often rub the wrong way, the day turned out to be a blessed Good Friday.

It was the day of the eighteenth meeting of the Association of Free Will Baptists in Brazil. The meeting was in honor of the twenty-five years Free Will Baptists had been in the country. Remembering, reminiscing, and learning about the bygone years proved to be a blessing, as we mentally saw the whole picture being filled in piece by piece. The struggles and blessings, the strengths and weaknesses, the defeats and victories, the failures and accomplishments turned out a picture perhaps somewhat marred by human failure, yet beautiful because it pictured the grace of God working in lives to build His church.

First missionary to Brazil, Dave Franks, spoke during the worship hour. He challenged Free Will Baptists to grow, to become involved, and to remain united to be able to produce more for the Lord's glory.

Slides showing the first missionaries and beginning of Free Will Baptist works helped to define the picture. The representatives from twelve works, who gave reports of history and progress, made even clearer the overall picture. Three works did not have representatives. Another bright spot was the testimonies of seven young men who were all in training for the ministry.

The first twenty-five years had become a completed picture—with renewed hopes, vision, aspirations, and desires to build for Christ's glory. Free Will Baptists in Brazil left the meeting with the challenge to put together a more beautiful picture during the next twenty-five years."

I met Gildete, a nurse and mother of two daughters, at the beauty shop. She was upset with her husband, and she was expressing her feelings to another person. Colonel José had become involved in transcendental meditation, so he spent much time meditating while seated on the ground in his backyard.

When she was a child and young person, Gildete had attended a Presbyterian Church and wanted things to be different. I'm sad to say she was talking to a spiritist, the wrong person to be able to help her. Even though the conversation was not including me, I made a way to enter. As soon as I began talking, Gildete said, "You must be a Christian. I would like to talk to you more about my husband."

Before we left the beauty shop, a time was marked to make a visit to the home of Colonel José and Gildete. Evidently, the colonel prepared himself for the visit. Very soon after the normal greetings, he began talking about the way meditation was helping him to find inner peace. Bobby and I sat listening for about two hours, only getting to say a word or two every now and then. We listened and he finally talked out. When it was time to go, Bobby simply said, "Colonel José, the only answer is in the Lord Jesus Christ, and I would like to share with you that message." Bobby and I had been patient in listening to him; thus, the result was an invitation to return the following week so that he could hear what we had to say.

The following are the testimonies of Colonel José and Gildete, showing the result of that meeting. She writes, "Receiving Jesus in my heart is such a great blessing in my life that I cannot explain it for lack of adequate words. I can only say it is marvelous how my life has been transformed. It is worth it all to have Jesus in my heart and find the real Christian life, which liberates." Shortly after he accepted Christ Colonel José wrote, "Jesus Christ, the living God's only Son freed me from darkness, a perturbed inner-life and mental agony, which was caused by my sins against the heavenly Father, His laws, and my fellowman. Blessed be the Lord, my God and my Savior, who came to my rescue."

§§

Missionary furloughs can have a devastating effect on new works. After returning to the field, we usually face a difficult time. One of the reasons is that a number of people may have dropped out and are not faithful to the Lord anymore. That particular furlough affected the youth. In fact, a Sunday school class no longer existed for the young people. The few left were involved in teaching ministries, except for two or three. The church asked me if I would become the teacher of the youth; that is why I reopened the class.

The very first Sunday the class met, I challenged the group of three students and one teacher to double in number as soon as possible. Prayers went up to the throne of grace on behalf of our desire. In a short time, the class no longer had four students, but eight. The challenge went out again to double as soon as possible.

Then one Sunday the three daughters of a doctor friend walked into my Sunday school class. On that particular Sunday, I gave an introduction to the Book of Galatians in preparation for an in-depth study of the letter to the Galatian believers. After the class, the three girls came up to me and wanted to know where I had gotten all my information. I told them that it came from a collection of studies for my classes in our Bible College, but I also recommended a book.

These girls were back the next Sunday, and the next, and the next. The class was on its way to doubling again.

Knowing that they were reared attending church, sometime later I asked them the reason they came to the Free Will Baptist Church. They told me that they liked using the Bible as a textbook and that they appreciated the in-depth studies. In the church where they had attended, the Bible was never in the hands of the teacher, and subjects discussed had very little basis in the Word of God. They said they were impressed with the Bible teaching done in our church and that never before had they sat under such teaching.

In three and a half years, that class reached its peak with forty-two on roll. I encouraged bringing visitors. About every Sunday, there were three or four visitors. Bringing people caused growth. Soon the younger brother of the three girls became a member of the class.

The growth of the Sunday school class caused the youth meeting held every Saturday night to grow. Many Saturdays there were sixty present for that meeting, so as the youth group grew the Sunday school class grew.

Out of the group came many leaders. Young people pared off and began dating as well. There were John and Renata, Jean and Flavia, Handrey and Flávia, Lincoln and Gislane, Rui and Deoliné who have become leaders in their respective churches. There were also Cesar and Cristiane, Guilherme and Fernanda, Rodrigo and Giuliana, and many others.

Strange! Yes, things were somewhat strange to the young, American exchange student. The smells, the cars, the homes, the language were all different.

Even the strangeness of the setting did not keep Jeff from feeling lucky, but did not realize how blessed. He had received placement in the home of a former exchange student who knew English well.

How strange his Brazilian brother was, especially in the part of religion. His church activities completely controlled him. That was too much! It was impossible for him to believe that Sergio, a young person, went to church on Thursday night, Saturday night, twice on Sunday, youth prayer group, youth choir practice, etc! In the eyes of the exchange student, Sergio was a fanatic! Anyway, he had never heard of a Free Will Baptist Church back home.

Jeff's busy schedule kept him occupied during the day, but nights while Sergio was involved in church activities he would think, *I can't see any need of all this. I'm a Christian. In the U.S., I went to church almost every Sunday morning. This business of talking and living Jesus all the time is not for me.*

Sergio extended many invitations to Jeff to attend church with him, but he always politely declined. After a few weeks Sergio's Sunday school teacher, who happened to be me, became concerned that Sergio had not been able to get Jeff to come to church. On Saturday I called Jeff, giving him an invitation. That time he used the excuse of his difficulty in understanding Portuguese. I did not allow that to be a reason. I politely offered to give my outline of the lesson to Jeff in English so he could follow along.

The next day Sergio walked in accompanied by Jeff. That got the ball rolling. From then on, at least once a week he was in church. He did not want to overdo a good thing.

Strange enough was the baptismal service—not only strange, but also impressive. Long into the night, Jeff and Sergio lay awake talking about a real Christian life. Language was somewhat a barrier, which made comprehension a little fuzzy.

Sergio did not allow the opportunity to pass without doing all he could. He asked Jeff if he would like to talk to me, his Sunday school teacher. He was willing.

No time was wasted. The next morning Sergio called me to see if I could talk with Jeff. Before hanging up the phone Sergio said, "We will be right over."

About ten minutes later the doorbell rang. I went to the door. There stood Sergio and Jeff. It was rather impressive to see tears flowing down Jeff's cheeks as he blurted out, "I thought I was a Christian, but I am not. Would you please tell me how to be saved?"

I took Jeff and Sergio into the dining room. Sitting at the dining table, I led Jeff into an acceptance of Christ as personal Savior. The puzzled look fled, and a peace and joy spread over the countenance of the young man.

The strange things Sergio did became the desire of Jeff's heart. Within one week, he had studied the Gospel of John. I was happy to provide Jeff with an English Bible since he did not have one with him in Brazil.

His last Saturday night in Brazil before returning to the states, Jeff brought a Bible study in Portuguese at the young people's meeting. That night he made these comments: "The Free Will Baptist Church in Ribeirão Preto, Brazil has been the first school of spiritual growth for me. I'm returning to the U.S., but I'll be back. I'll be back as a missionary."

Two years or so later a missionary couple, who had served a few years with the Mennonite church in the city of Ribeirão Preto, came back to

Brazil for a visit. They made a point to come through Ribeirão Preto. On Saturday, we received a phone call from them. They wanted us to get together with them for a meal on Sunday.

Just before their visit to Brazil, they had gone to the training camp of Youth with a Mission. They began to tell Bobby and me about their experience at the training camp. For their meals, they ate with those in training. With two extra places at a particular table, and an invitation extended, they sat with the group of young people.

The young people introduced themselves and gave a little information about themselves as well. The missionary couple did the same. They told about having served in Brazil. Jeff was at that particular table. Immediately he asked, "Where in Brazil?" These missionaries gave the various places where they had served, ending with Ribeirão Preto. Jeff came back with, "Ribeirão Preto! Do you happen to know Bobby and Geneva Poole?" He then proceeded to tell them how he came to the Lord and had promised to return to Brazil as a missionary.

How precious it was to hear Jeff's story. The thought of our precious friend, Jeff, in the northern part of Brazil working with Youth with a Mission, was indeed a blessing. Great things God has done and the glory of His grace evidenced once again.

§§

In one phase of the developing of the evangelistic efforts of the young people, they requested that I, their Sunday school teacher, help them to learn how to present the plan of salvation. The cogs of my mind began to turn. I wanted to give them a practical lesson along with the plan itself. God gave me a solution.

A date was set about a month in advance for the practical lesson. I did not give the purpose, but just simply asked the students to pray for that particular day. They were to bring an unsaved friend with them to church to be able to participate in my Sunday school class. The rest of the class would have another teacher for the Sunday school hour. Each Sunday I reminded the students of the special day and asked them not to forget to pray for that day and to bring an unsaved friend.

At that time class attendance was averaging around twenty-six. On the special project day, thirteen members brought thirteen visitors who were not Christians. These remained with me doing the teaching. After the introduction of each friend, I started the lesson. I took the class through the Roman's Road, step-by-step. I allowed each student to explain to his friend each step. Then at the end of the lesson, I had the students to ask their friends if they would like to accept Jesus as Savior. Several prayed that day.

Among those present was Jeancarlo, Samuel's friend. Jeancarlo, known as Jean, was so impressed with the class that he kept coming back. Shortly thereafter, he went to youth camp with the group from First Free Will Baptist Church in Ribeirão. At camp, he made a public decision for Christ.

Every Sunday he was back in Sunday school and the night service as well. I remember talking to Bobby about a particular young person who seemed to eat up every opportunity to learn.

Soon I learned that Jean's mother and father were separated. I also learned that it was his norm to stay with his father on weekends. He soon told his dad that he needed to be in Ribeirão on Saturday nights and Sundays. Jean grew spiritually and soon developed into a leader.

Upon graduation from high school, Jean wanted to enter our Bible College in the First Church. His mother thought it absurd to go to school to study the Bible. Finally, she allowed him to go if he would take business administration at a secular college at the same time. Jean enrolled in both colleges. He went to college in the morning and at night and studied all afternoon. God worked in Jean and he did not give up either school, thus in the same year he graduated with two bachelor of arts degrees.

During Jean's last year of college, he busied himself in the church in Jaboticabal. When he finished college, he accepted the call to be the pastor of the church. Under his leadership the church has grown from about forty to over two hundred in attendance. Because of the growth, the church took on a full-time assistant pastor.

During a missionary conference, Jean and Flavia had their hearts challenged for the country of Ireland. They brought their desire back to their church and, after much prayer, the church granted Jean a two-year leave of absence with pay to work in the country of Ireland. There he and his family won the hearts of the Irish people in the area where they worked. Because of them, there is a bond between the Brazilian Free Will Baptist churches in our area and the Irish people.

After cancer surgery, when I was just beginning the chemotherapy, Bobby and I were at Walmart. We met Lincoln and Gislaine, who talked to us about having "a get-together" of the ones in the youth Sunday school class and the youth group from the early 1980's. We set a Saturday night about two weeks later for a time of fellowship of the group.

I was a bit saddened about my health situation and perhaps a little self-conscious since I had lost all of my hair that week and was wearing a wig for the first time. Both Bobby and I were a little let down and saddened when we arrived at the placed the meeting was to be held and no one was there. After thinking about the situation, we called our son's mother-in-law, who gave us the correct location we were to be—the first Free Will Baptist church we started. Bobby and I decided that because of our usual punctuality, we had been purposely sent to the wrong place to cause us to delay a little, so most of the people would be at the church when we arrived.

Our spirits were definitely uplifted as we entered the church where about one hundred and fifty people had gathered. Even with such a short notice, people had driven from all directions to get to the meeting. Many came from as far as five hours away.

It was soon evident that the meeting was in our honor.

The program started with the music director of those days, leading the group in some of the music sung during those years when we were together in the church. The group sung beautifully, and it was good for everyone to reminisce a little. After the uplifting music, came a time for anyone who so desired to give a testimony.

Person after person went to the front and spoke words of greeting and then of the years they had been under the teachings and leadership of Pastor Bobby and Dona Geni (Bobby and me). Many of them stated things in our lives that had been a blessing to them. One even asked for forgiveness for the time he had been part of the evangelism class of seven students and six of them refused to memorize the Scripture verses. You can guess the results. Yes, six students failed.

As one after another spoke, there were certain things said that we still remember. A number of times the person said there were two things about us they could not forget that had been an influence in their lives. The two things were our love for people and our love for the Word of God. They had become what they had become because of the love shown to them and because of our teaching them to love and obey the Word of God. What a difference those things had made in their lives!

Another pleasant surprise came at the time to close out the program. The music director called all choir members to the front to sing two of the special numbers they had sung many years before. They harmonized beautifully. What sweet music that was to our ears and to God's as well, as it went up and circled around His throne.

Finally, the group participated in a reception given in our honor.

Greatly to be praised is our Lord, who did a work of grace in all those lives. It is a blessing to know they are faithfully serving in many parts of this great land of Brazil for the glory of His grace. Great things God had done!

The telephone rang! That time it was the church's big talker. She was one who wanted to help others so much until she often spoiled everything by being *too* helpful. "No" was never an answer to what she wanted. That explains in part the refusal of her request.

She had wanted the church to pay the rent for a young couple she had just met and buy them some groceries to tide them through until she could help the young man find a job.

Bobby said that he could give personally and perhaps others in the church would do the same. Immediately she set out to raise the needed funds. Within a few hours, she had the money in hand to help the couple, who just after being married had come into town in search of a brighter future.

At that moment things were rather dismal for the couple, not only because of their lack of food but also because they were about to lose the apartment they had rented.

The names "Hemmer and Yeda" had no magic when they sometime earlier had hung out their sign as tailors of women's apparel. Oh, yes, they had had a few customers, but not enough to get along. What were they going to do?

Then Rachel came into their lives. She not only helped them financially by the gifts and finding Hemmer a job, but she also told them about the Free Will Baptist Church.

Rachel called Bobby and gave him all the details about Hemmer and Yeda with a request that he and I make a visit. She had gotten the church people involved, and they had begun to pray that God would be honored and glorified through the couple.

The night came for our first visit. We were impressed with Hemmer and Yeda by their cordial welcome, their intelligent conversation, and their gentle manners. They certainly were not the ordinary type of people who asked for handouts.

That night was the turning point in their lives, for they both accepted Christ as their Savior. It had been easy to turn the conversation to spiritual things. After their prayer, they both became radiant with joy because of their newfound faith.

On Sunday they were at the First Free Will Baptist Church in Ribeirão Preto, and before long, out of sheer joy for learning, they both entered the Bible College at the church. As they went deeper and deeper into the Word, the Holy Spirit began to impress upon Antonio (Hemmer was his professional name) the need for pastors, to which he yielded himself.

Not yet thirty years of age, Antonio had already become very much a part of the history of the Free Will Baptist denomination in Brazil. He received a B.A. degree in theology from our Brazilian Bible College in Ribeirão Preto in 1982. He became the first moderator of the Brazilian Association of Free Will Baptists and began the newspaper of the association, which circulated among Free Will Baptists in Brazil. He eventually became a professor at the Bible College from where he had graduated, and the pastor of the First Free Will Baptist Church in Ribeirão Preto as well.

Love for people and a desire to help them spiritually was the heartbeat of Antonio and Yeda. It was not strange that they rode the bus for an hour and a half to the city of Franca, to be able to have a meeting in his mother's home with family and friends whom he desired to win to Christ, many of whom have since become believers.

If anything needed to be done, all you needed to do was ask Antonio. He may have been the busiest person in the church, but he managed to get it done with that perfection which was definitely a characteristic of all his work.

Antonio and Yeda had many friends in Franca with whom they wanted to share the good news of salvation. They talked with Rubens, a physics teacher, and his wife Angelica about opening their home for a service in Franca. They agreed, so Bobby, along with Antonio and Yeda, made the hour's drive to Franca once a month for a while. It was at that time that Rubens and Angelica accepted the Lord.

Shortly after their conversion, Rubens and Angelica moved to a town about twenty minutes from Ribeirão Preto. After their move, they began attending the First Free Will Baptist Church where Bobby and I were serving. They have been a blessing to the work of the Lord participating in as many of the church activities as possible, serving as Sunday school teachers, Sunday school superintendent, and in dramas and children's activities. They were and are examples to be observed and followed.

God has used that family in two of the new works started in Ribeirão Preto, the Second Church and the Marincek work. It has been a blessing to have people like Rubens and Angelica, who are willing to change churches to help begin a new work.

Now their children have grown up and two of the three are very active in the work of the Lord. Andraus is using his music ability to serve in the First Free Will Baptist Church in Ribeirão Preto. Ariádine is active in the Marincek church and, at present, is a Sunday school teacher and the program chairman for the Women's Auxiliary, and directs Friends Club, the children's outreach program of the church. Ariádine is treasurer of the Marincek Church as well.

Rui, a high-school student, heard the announcement about a Christian music festival. The details remained in his mind; write the lyric, compose the music, make a tape and enter it. The committee was to choose thirty-six of these taped compositions for the festival, with a live performance of each singing group.

One day several Christian friends were talking with Rui. Just to see their reaction he mentioned the festival. They decided to pray about it. To enter the festival might hurt their testimony, which they certainly did not want.

The young men prayed and God began to work in their minds. Therefore, before long they had two Christian songs ready to record. All they asked God was that He use the music and their lives for His glory.

Some days later, the results of the recorded selections became available. Somewhat to their surprise, one of their songs was on the list. With a desire to be used for God's glory, an ensemble of the seven participants was formed that earnestly sought His direction. They prayed, "Show us, Lord, how we can be used to bring glory to your name."

The first night of the festival came and did not catch them off guard. Since that would probably be their only chance, they took advantage of the opportunity by giving out gospel tracts as they waited their turn to sing.

God provided another chance. Just prior to their time to sing, the festival was discontinued until the next evening.

The next evening the group went even better prepared to take advantage of the opportunities to witness, which included mimeographed copies of testimonies of what the Lord Jesus meant to them.

The ensemble gave their presentation and awaited the results. To their surprise, they had made the classification and would be entering the finals.

They continued to pray that God would use their song for His glory, and He did! As they sang their song about the Lord Jesus Christ there was a holy hush on the crowd. God was doing a great work in these young people.

Even greater was their surprise when the master of ceremonies announced them as the winner. Yes, the ensemble of seven young people who desired to bring glory to God had won. The trophy was given to Rui who turned to the audience and said, "We do not want the glory. We give that to the Lord Jesus Christ."

※

Four Christian young people from the Free Will Baptist Church, who participated in a choir of one of the well-known music teachers in the city, were quite perplexed. They did not know what to do.

One of the songs chosen for the citywide choir festival was "Macumba," a song carrying the name of one of the spiritist movements in Brazil.

Would God be pleased if they sang that song? Would not just singing it be a testimony against the Lord Jesus Christ? These and many other questions popped into their minds as their hearts yearned to have an answer.

Two of the young men went to the choir director and asked that she remove that particular song. Even though the director was a Christian, she laughed and continued practicing it. She also said that the song had nothing to do with religion, but that they would be singing it for its cultural value.

Very distraught about the effect on their own testimony, they came to me, their Sunday school teacher. "What can we do?" was their earnest plea.

One suggested that they all four combine to quit if she did not change that song. To lose four important voices in the choir would be quite a blow.

I explained that if they did such a thing they must be ready to accept the consequences. Then I suggested that they really put the problem before the Lord and give Him a chance to solve it. The young people prayed. The women's prayer group asked God to intervene. The whole church prayed! Of course, an answer came!

The choir members were unable to learn the music; therefore the choir director chose Psalm 150 to be sung in its place. Psalm 150 is a song of praise, and the four young people sang it as a testimony of God's greatness. Some of the words they sang were, "Praise ye the Lord. Praise God…let everything that hath breath praise the Lord. Praise ye the Lord!"

※

In 1981, when Guilherme was fifteen years old, he began attending the Free Will Baptist church. Joel, a friend in his class at school, had invited him to an ice-cream supper. There were two reasons he went. The first one was his desire to have a good time, and the second one was to see some of the girls he had been attracted to who attended the church.

It was in the Free Will Baptist church that he heard for the first time Bible truths like, "For God so loved the world that he gave His only begotten Son…." Until that time, Guilherme had never received any spiritual instruction nor had he ever been told the important things of God, because he was from a family with no spiritual direction.

As time passed Guilherme accepted the Lord as his Savior, followed the Lord in baptism, and became a member of the church. He and his grandmother were the only ones in his family who were Christians. A year later at the family retreat Guilherme's sister, Giuliana, accepted Christ as her Savior.

Problems in their home were terrible. Finally, in 1983 his parents separated. His dad, along with the younger siblings, went to live in the northern part of Brazil. Guilherme and the older brother stayed with their mother in Ribeirão Preto. During that time, Guilherme was faithful in church attendance. However, when his dad died in 1986, his spiritual weakness caused him to leave the things of his faith to the side. He blamed God for his father's death. He accused the church family of not giving him the help he needed at that particular time as well. Later he wrote, "As I look back on that time, I know I was wrong."

Soon after graduation from college in 1994, Guilherme married Fernanda, one of our daughters in the faith. At first things went well in their marriage. But Guilherme left God out of his life and he began to drink quite heavily. Within a short period of time, both his sister and mother died. With their deaths, he went deeper into sin. He became a drug user.

Guilherme was a hard worker and had accomplished much, but he was so empty. He searched for pleasure outside of the marriage, which ended up destroying another home. With his Christian wife out of his life, things got even worse. He was out of control. He fought in the bars, searched out drug pushers, and soon tried to take his own life.

This is Guilherme's testimony given in his own words.

"In March of 2001, I was in my darkroom alone, hallucinating and trying to hang myself. Life did not have any meaning. I had no desire to live. I was unable to sleep. I had searched for pleasure and found none. I began to cry and desperately ask God for help. I asked Him to help me die or show me what was happening. Fernanda's words came to my memory. She had told me that she thought it strange that when I was an adolescent I was so good and kind, but as an adult, I was evil and full of myself. I also remembered how that when in church I could handle the bad things that came upon me. Based on this, I searched for and found my old Bible. With this Bible in front of me, I sat for hours reading all of the verses that I had underlined. These were verses that I had learned in Sunday school, at camp, in the worship services, and in the youth meetings as well. For three days, I stayed at home reading the Bible; I did not even leave to get food. I prayed and asked God to forgive me. God helped me understand many things. He showed me that He forgives no matter what we have done, and He showed me what I was—nothing, clay, weak in the faith, unwise, and a rebellious son. Finally, He made me understand that He is the creator and Lord as well as Savior."

Some time has passed and Guilherme has left the intensive care unit, spiritually speaking that is. Working on his doctorate degree, he now lives in Spain where he faithfully attends church. He wrote, "Today I live by faith in the Lord Jesus Christ! I cannot understand why God had so much mercy, but I want to express my gratitude all the rest of my life. He has given me another chance. I have victory in Christ."

❧❧

Marcia had had contact with the evangelical church through an aunt before her family moved from a satellite city near Brasilia, the national capital, to Ribeirão Preto. But she had never accepted Christ as her personal Savior.

Juscelino, her husband, was drinking more heavily. Things at home were not going so well. She hated to have their three sons see their dad in his drunken stupors. That situation helped drive her to search for a church. She found First Free Will Baptist Church where she began attending and soon accepted Christ as her Savior.

Marcia's family became her concern, so she prayed and invited. Soon Juscelino accepted the invitation to go to church with her. The first time he entered the church he did not simply walk in; he was so drunk that he staggered in. However, it was sobering what he heard, so he kept going. Soon he accepted Christ as his personal Savior. That decision was real and powerful. He testifies that from that moment on he has never had a desire for an alcoholic drink. God had taken the desire away. God did that great thing in Juscelino's life!

Marcia was indeed happy, but her oldest son refused to go to church with them. She did not give up; invitations continued. Finally, one Sunday night Lucas accepted the invitation and he went to church. Instead of paying attention to the service, his attention went in the direction of the open ceiling, which housed some undesirable creatures, birds and bats.

At home that night Marcia approached Lucas. She wanted to know what he thought about the service. All he could talk about was the birds and bats. In spite of his lack of desire to learn from the Scriptures, he returned with his family the next Sunday. Once again it was evident he had not been paying attention.

After the third Sunday night visit, as they walked into their apartment, Lucas said, "You know I liked what Preacher John said." Marcia was overjoyed at the fact that God was answering her prayers.

Lucas continued going, accepted Christ, became active in the ministries of the church, and enrolled in the Bible College held at the church. In 2007, he received a B. A. degree in theology, and in 2008 he was ordained as a Free Will Baptist minister. He is a very promising dedicated young man.

During our years in Brazil, Bobby and I have lived in one city and done most of our work there. In reality, God has used us as instruments to start four churches, but only three of them are still in existence today.

The third church started was in the rich area of the city and lasted for ten years. Funds to get the work started came from friends who were members of the Presbyterian Church in Lake City, S. C. They were people who believed God could do great things in Brazil.

To open the new work, we planned and gave a Sunday afternoon tea in order to get to know people near the church, to show them the facilities, and to explain our desire to plant a church in the area. That afternoon three families from the First Free Will Baptist Church came and expressed a desire to help in the work. What a blessing it was to have a nucleus to begin that new work!

That rich area was one of the hardest areas in which to work since many of the people had no interest in learning about God. They could solve all their problems with their money. Bobby and I count it a privilege to have had the opportunity of working in that suburb. We worked hard and learned many lessons during that time. With the help of the church people and two summer missionaries, we canvassed the area and each month during that year we put a different illustrated gospel message into the mailboxes.

During at least two of our stateside assignments that work survived fine under local leadership. Each time Bobby and I came back into the work with encouraged hearts to reach people in that area for the Lord. The church grew. By the time of our next prolonged absence, the congregation was running about fifty.

That absence did not work out too well. By the time we returned, more than half of the congregation had disappeared.

From that time until the work closed on its tenth anniversary, the church just could not get up the momentum for a spurt of growth. A negative spirit about keeping a church in that area permeated the group. Those attitudes became prevalent while we were away. Another element involved in the work being closed was a financial one. Rent was extremely expensive, and the small congregation was under too much stress to come up with the necessary amount each month. Closing the doors of that church was one of the hardest things we have had to do in our entire missionary career; yet we are certain that Romans 8:28 is true. "And we know that all things work together for good to them that love God, to them who are the called according to his purpose."

The efforts put forth in that area of the city were not in vain, however. In fact, the Second Church started the Marincek work during its period of existence. After Carlos Jayne's graduation from our Bible College at First Free Will Baptist Church, he and his family started attending the Second Church. He was ready to get into a work where he would be the pastor or leader. Bobby asked him if he would be willing to open a work in the housing development of Marincek. He and his family were thrilled about the idea.

Factors involved in choosing Marincek for a new work were, there was no evangelical church in the area, and there were several people who had been saved in the Free Will Baptist Church living in that area. In fact, one family was taking two buses to be able to attend Second Free Will Baptist Church. It would be a blessing for them to have a Free Will Baptist church nearby.

How the work would be financed was another problem. We came to the agreement that Carlos would need to serve as part-time pastor and work to support his family. The Second Church would provide for housing, a meeting place, and the regular monthly bills.

Bobby and I had received a small inheritance after the death of my mother in 1988. What could we do with that money which would be an extension of my parents love for the Lord and His work in Brazil? My parents had given monthly to our account from the time we went to the field until their deaths. After buying a piano for the Second Church, we used most of the inheritance to purchase a house in the Marincek subdivision, remodeled it, and converted the backyard space into a meeting hall.

In a short time, Carlos and Valeria had been able to reach out to many people. Sad to say, in time people became dissatisfied and left the church. Carlos had an opportunity to go to another Free Will Baptist church, so Marincek was left without a leader. It was just about that time that the Second Church closed, so Bobby and I took over the new work. Our first night in Marincek we had only seven people attend the service, but soon we were able to reach out to some of the people that Carlos had worked with and bring them back to the church. A new phase of our lives had begun.

※

Celso had been brought up attending a Baptist Church. Maria Helena had been reared a Catholic, but after she and Celso were married, she started attending church with him. She accepted Christ as her personal Savior, but after a time she and Celso became lax in their faithfulness to the Lord and finally dropped out of church altogether.

Then one day, through a neighbor's invitation, Celso went back to church and became active. Maria Helena went with him, but did not feel comfortable in the charismatic atmosphere of that church. The emotional highs were not her mode of worship, so she stopped going.

Through an invitation of a friend, she began attending the Marincek Free Will Baptist Church, returned to the Lord, and became a faithful worker. She only began attending regularly with her husband's permission. The family was divided. Celso, Jr. and Jaqueline, two of their older children, both attended different congregations. Joel did not attend any place. The two small children, ages 3 and 8, were pulled in two directions between their dad and their mom. Celso would insist that they go with him at least once on Sunday, but they wanted to go with their mother. They enjoyed the atmosphere and the various activities including Sunday school, children's church, and Friends Club of the Free Will Baptist Church. Naturally, that brought conflict between Celso and Maria Helena.

Celso would come by for Maria Helena after church, sit in his car, and have nothing to do with the people of the church, especially the missionaries. He looked as if he could bite a nail in two. It seemed as if he thought the Free Will Baptist Church was the cause of all his problems. That situation continued for two years or longer. Jaqueline began attending the Marincek Free Will Baptist Church. Celso, Jr. married his girlfriend who was pregnant, but not too long after the baby was born, they separated. Joel began hanging out with the wrong crowd and became involved with drugs. The family was not doing well at all. Conflicts between Celso and Maria Helena were mounting each day. Because of attitudes, the home was in turmoil.

Early one morning before Bobby and I were out of bed, Jaqueline called to let us know that Joel had committed suicide. As soon as we could get dressed, we went over to their home to be with Maria Helena. Celso's pastor was there when we arrived, but left almost immediately. Bobby and I stayed and helped them in their hour of great need. The funeral was that afternoon; thus, all that day either Bobby and I or the assistant pastor and his wife were with them. We provided food for the family, which is not the custom in Brazil. Celso's pastor did not return until about fifteen minutes before the body was taken to the cemetery. That was hard to understand, but perhaps it was difficult for him to deal with a suicide case. Bobby and I had learned that in these difficult times the only thing that can be done is to show love and concern for those who are still alive; and that we tried to do.

After investigation, it was determined that Joel did not kill himself, but he had been pushed from the sixth floor of a building in construction, which was possibly the result of his involvement with drug pushers.

Bobby and I do not know what influence our being present with the hurting parents had upon Celso. After we visited Celso and Maria Helena a couple of times that week, Celso called his pastor telling him that his family was more important than going to a particular church, and he had decided to attend with Maria Helena. He also told Maria Helena his decision, and then added, "But I am never going to become a Baptist." It seemed apparent that he felt spiritually superior, perhaps because of his charismatic background.

As the months passed, Celso began to fit into the mode of worship at the Free Will Baptist Church. Occasionally Bobby asked him to speak. He was a good preacher with messages full of content. Therefore, little by little he became a part of the church. Then, the last night before Bobby and I left for a stateside assignment, he asked Bobby if he could say a word. He told the church that he had not even told Maria Helena, but he had decided that he wanted to become a member so he could get involved more with the work of the Lord through the church.

Celso has become involved. In fact, there are few people who have the courage to speak out for the Lord every opportunity afforded them and such ability to make opportunities as Celso does. He was moving a piano for a priest from one apartment building to another. When Celso arrived, the priest asked him if he would have some breakfast with him. Celso accepted, but before he ate, he asked if he could pray. The priest granted permission, so Celso prayed aloud. After breakfast, Celso moved the piano and was on his way out of the apartment, when the priest called him back and asked him to pray once again before leaving. Celso prayed and talked to him for a while about the Christ that he serves.

Celso shared with Bobby about an interesting opportunity to witness. He was leaving the center of town going back to his place of work when he felt impressed of the Lord to go by one of the hospitals to speak with a friend. He prayed asking God to supply him a place to park close to the hospital if He really wanted him to stop. When he arrived, there was a vacant parking space right in front of the door. He went in and told the receptionist that he had an appointment (given by God) with a certain director, so he lost no time and went right in. The conversation revealed that the director was contemplating suicide. Celso was able to help him in that difficult time of his life.

It has been wonderful to see the changes that have taken place in the life of each individual of that family, except Celso, Jr. who still has not come back to the Lord. They are a happy united family working together for the cause of the Lord. That is what love, prayer, patience, and teaching can do. Ideas changed and lives transformed. Praise God! God is doing great things!

Sad to say, as time passed Celso accepted some books that got him to thinking once again of the charismatic ideas of health and wealth. Slowly and slyly he began incorporating these ideas into his home Bible studies and then into the church. Our steadfast Free Will Baptist people became upset with the change in his teaching, especially when we were not present. Bobby had long talks with Celso about Free Will Baptist doctrine. He did not defend his point of view, but seemed to become more convinced that he could and should change the church. He became more open with his charismatic doctrines. Bobby decided that he could not allow him to preach anymore. Because he could not preach he left the church. That time his wife decided to go with him, even though she did not agree with his doctrine. She said that she was afraid of what Celso might do.

Today Celso is enrolled in Free Will Baptist Bible College at the First Free Will Baptist Church. Bobby and I both give him classes. Evidently he realizes his need to go deeper into the Word. We are still praying for him and working with him. We trust he can still work with Free Will Baptists. A few months ago, Celso and Maria Helena invited us to their home for a meal. We had a lovely evening with them and are still friends, but have our doctrinal differences.

The field council in Brazil voted on and passed a motion to sell the camp property. It was hard for Bobby and me to accept the idea of not having a place for camps, even though we could understand the thinking of the other missionaries who lived so far away that the camp was of little use to them.

Bobby and I began to pray and try to figure out a way for us to purchase the property. One idea was to sell part of it to help pay for it. A realtor friend from Jaboticabal had offered his services to make part of the property into a housing development. With that in mind, we made an offer to purchase the property. At that time things did not work out. So we took that as God's sign to forget the idea of keeping the campgrounds under Free Will Baptists. Nevertheless, we did not stop praying.

Because of the paperwork involved, two years later the property had not sold, but buyers were waiting with the money in hand. Bobby and I were more saddened when we heard that plans were to demolish the camp, to build a motel—to the Brazilians, a place of prostitution—or turn the property into a housing development.

Attitudes seem to change among the missionaries. Bobby and I were in the states when the field chairman in Brazil asked us if we were still interested in purchasing the property. Of course, the answer was yes. We were returning to the field for the annual field council meeting, at which time Bobby was to make an offer.

At that meeting, Bobby suggested that we divide the camp property into three sections to be sold separately. Bobby and I would purchase more than half of the property, which was everything needed for the camp to continue to function. That proposal was accepted, but with the stipulation that these transactions be done within four months. Knowing how slowly things move along in Brazil that seemed impossible, but with God nothing is impossible. God did great things! The buyers, all Free Will Baptists, appeared and the deal went through.

We retired under Social Security about that same time, so we borrowed the money and paid the loan off with our Social Security income. July of

2007 was the last payment. God is wonderful and greatly to be praised! Great things God has done.

§§

Since the mission had been discussing the sale of the campgrounds for about ten years, the camp administrator did not do anything on the buildings, which was not an absolute necessity. In fact, the property was in a very rundown state. It really needed a face-lift.

Even while still paying for the camp, we have been able to renovate six of the buildings and build a new tabernacle. More than thirty-six hundred plants have been set out. Two different missionaries said that they have never seen the place look so pretty, and they both had lived on the property in past years.

Through that experience, we have learned to leave everything in God's hands and He will have His will done. That camp property is an expensive project for one missionary couple, but a blessing to the works in our area.

§§

When she was only five years old Paula started attending the Free Will Baptist Church with her grandmother.

During the night service, the smaller children stayed in the nursery. Paula did not want to stay with those children. One night, with permission, she went downstairs to the meeting hall. She did not want her Grandmother to discover that she was there so she sat on a bench in the back.

That night the subject of the sermon was hell, the place of punishment. Paula became interested in what Bobby was saying, so she perked up and listened. She decided she did not want to go to that place; thus, when he gave the invitation she went forward and accepted Christ as her personal Savior.

Since that time Paula has been very active in the work of the Lord. She is now a grown woman. God has continued to use her.

Paula always had a real interest in studying English. When she was a teenager, every opportunity afforded, she helped to interpret for American groups that came to Brazil. Over the years, she has developed quite a knowledge and usage of the English language, which has become an open door for her.

Paula is using her ability to teach English as a means to an end. Teaching English opened the door for her to enter China where she is a testimony for Christ. The First Free Will Baptist Church of Ribeirão Preto, her home church, has been her sending and supporting organization.

Paula has recently withdrawn herself from under the direction of the church, but still serves in China.

§§

During our stateside assignment in 2008, we went to South Carolina for our usual visits to the churches in my home state. Since we were traveling in our RV and Lebanon Free Will Baptist Church had extended a standing invitation to take advantage of the hookup at the church, we parked there. It was a joy to be with the people of one of the churches I considered my home church. During several stateside assignments, our boys and I attended Lebanon along with my parents. When we did not have a speaking engagement, we enjoyed the services and fellowship with them. That was great because it gave us an opportunity to stay parked in one spot and travel out from there.

One night soon after everyone from the Spanish church had left, someone knocked on our door. At first, Bobby talked to the person with the door closed; but since it was a young girl, he opened the door. She said that she ran out of gasoline and needed to make a phone call. She gave Bobby the number and he punched it in and handed the phone to her. She talked a bit and then gave the phone back to him. She was only a short distance away and Bobby was still talking to her when a man came around the back of the RV and jumped him, catching him from the back. He had a club in his hand with which he was trying to hit Bobby. When I saw what was going on, I grabbed a big metal flashlight. As I stepped down out of the RV, a man jumped me. Someway he got the flashlight, but did not hold onto it. It rolled some distance away where he could not hold on to me and retrieve the flashlight. I believe an angel of God was fighting for me and rolled the flashlight far enough away that the man could not reach it. With all my strength, I began pounding him with my fists and screaming.

Then I realized there was no use for me to scream, because we were out in the country where the nearest house was a distance down the road. No one would be near enough to hear me. He kept saying, "Get in. Get into the RV." Naturally, I did not obey, but sat down on the second step. I was not going in and decided if he went in, he would have to climb over me or lift me into the RV.

Then I believe the Holy Spirit put in my mind the need to pray. I calmed down and started praying in a loud commanding voice. I said something to this effect: "Dear God, you know we need Your protection. Please be with us. Protect us from these who desire to harm us." Then I looked the man in the eye and said, "You are allowing the devil to use you, and I ask you in the name of the Lord Jesus to stop right now." He continued holding on to my arms and trying to make me get into the RV. I continued to pray and finally I said, "I demand you in the name of the Lord Jesus to stop right now." He froze, but still kept me captive by holding onto my arms.

Finally, Bobby got the club and "clobbered" the man fighting with him several times. He fled saying, "Come on, let's go." He picked up Bobby's Palm Pilot that had fallen to the ground and fled. The one holding me fled with him.

We both jumped into the RV and made a phone call to 911 and to the pastor. In less than five minutes, 911 responded to our call and arrived at the church. Then the pastor and several other men from the church came.

Evidently, the man who fought with Bobby bit Bobby's thumb, which took a while to heal. All the other scratches were minor.

Police were still on their chase in the woods, with dogs to catch the intruders, when we went in to prepare ourselves for a night of rest. We thanked God for His protection over us during the ordeal. We asked God for continued protection as well. We prayed that something we did or said God would use to help those men to stop that kind of crime, to see the need of accepting Christ, and to allow God to work in their lives.

I could go on and on giving stories and testimonies, but the ones included are sufficient enough to see how God has worked and is continuing to work in our lives and ministry.

Naturally, not all the people won to the Lord have gotten into the work, nor have all of them continued to remain close to Him. There are many sad accounts of those who have strayed away, but we prefer to dwell on the victories rather than the failures, disappointments, and heartaches.

Bobby and I are sure there are people in many parts of Brazil now serving the Lord because they accepted the Lord and got their beginning of spiritual growth in one of the Free Will Baptist churches in Ribeirão Preto. For instance, in just the last year from the First Free Will Baptist Church, two families have moved to the state of Bahia, one to Santa Catarina, and one to Minas Gerais. Bobby and I feel that they are grounded sufficiently in the Word to continue in their service for the Lord. In fact, several of them were students in the Bible College of First Church.

There has been a great change in the number of Christians in the country during the time we have lived in Brazil. When we went there were less than two percent Christians, but today there is somewhere approximately twenty-five percent. As we look back upon our ministry, we are sure that only the Lord knows what has been accomplished because we answered God's call upon our lives to work for Him in Brazil. We have always considered ourselves as only instruments with a desire for God to use us to accomplish great things for the glory of His grace.

07.
A DARK LAND

"Come out of the man, thou unclean spirit."
MARK 5:8

Brazil is considered to have the world's largest Catholic population. The Portuguese settlers who first colonized Brazil were Catholics; therefore, Brazil was founded on the Catholic faith. Centuries passed before the protestant faith was able to gain a firm footing in the society. As the freed slaves became incorporated into the society, another religion, Spiritism, became very popular. A person can be both a Catholic and a Spiritist. Along the many years of its history, these beliefs have led the Brazilians to become a superstitious people. The superstitious mind can easily fall into the clutches of satanic powers, which opens the door for demon possession. Satan is real and alive in Brazil. Anyone in the service of the true and living God soon realizes that.

Much of demon possession is subtle, because Satan does not want people to recognize it as such. In earlier days, there were more open manifestations of demon possession than today. That does not mean there is less today. With so many drugs, which open the mind to allow Satan to dominate, there is probably more today; but the demons do not manifest themselves as readily. Perhaps Satan does a lot of camouflaging so the Christian will not believe demon possession exists today, nor recognize it so it can be dealt with it for what it really is.

There is a danger to blame things on the devil when it is just human nature or human fabrication. At one particular time in Brazil, we knew pastors of other denominations who became obsessed with demon activity. One pastor, who had served as an evangelist a number of times for the First Free Will Baptist Church, became one of them. He was a guest in our home. He began to accuse many people of things they were doing that were signs of demonic activity. He said the girl working in our home was demon possessed, and she was sending those demons to others by the way she pointed her finger at everyone. He also told us that a certain potted plant I had was a place for demons to house while they were looking for a body for their abode. That plant stayed around quite a while after that, but that pastor did not receive another invitation to work with us. We should not take lightly demonic powers, nor should we take lightly God's power for victory and protection over demonic powers. Remember Satan is powerful, but God is all-powerful. First John 4:4 says, "Greater is he that is in you, than he that is in the world."

Our first recognition of dealing face-to-face with a demon-possessed person came during our very first term of missionary service. Bobby had made several visits to that particular home where there was a young man whose parents said was mentally perturbed. Bobby invited the young man to come to church. He accepted the invitation. The night he was present, the Holy Spirit was working in a special way, which brought conviction upon the young man about his need of a Savior. During the invitation, he went forward to accept Christ as his personal Savior.

When he reached the front of the church, his countenance changed and he began to speak in a guttural voice, using the third person. It was evident that it was the demon using the voice box of his victim. How shocking it was to hear the deep guttural voice uttering, "He does not need Jesus Christ. What he needs is our lady," referring to the Virgin Mary. He kept repeating those words becoming more emotionally involved each time until he finally became violent. The whole church realized what was going on, so Bobby asked the men leaders to go with him into a classroom, and he took the young man with them.

Previously, Bobby had been warned of the strength of a demon-possessed person, so he took the necessary precautions of taking several men with him and taking off his tie as well. While they were dealing with the young man, the entire church did very serious praying. They wanted the man freed and the all-powerful, true, and living God to protect every person present because, when the demons leave a person, they begin looking for another abode. Apparently, victory came that night.

When dealing with demons three things can happen. First, the person freed from the clutches of demons continues to resist satanic forces to remain free. Second, the liberated person does not resist when the demon returns bringing with him other demons; therefore, his second state is worse than the first. Third, the demon says he is leaving, but he is a liar, and he never leaves; thus, the person continues to be demon possessed.

In the case of that young man, it was difficult to know whether the second or third state applied. He did not come back to church. During a visit a few of days later, his family let Bobby know that he was put in a mental hospital and they no longer desired his help.

Bobby and I had made a visit to Dona Rosalina's home and met her husband. She later told us how he was very much involved in Spiritism. He would go into trances, speak in a foreign language, and break up everything in the house, but not realize he was doing it. These actions were evident signs of demon possession.

Another day, when Bobby was visiting Palmiro, he had the opportunity to explain to him the salvation message. As he did, Bobby heard noises outside as if someone was throwing rocks against something. As he listened, he was convinced by the sound that someone was bombarding his car with rocks. Bobby got up and looked out, but saw no one near the car. He continued with his explanation of the plan of salvation to the unsaved man, but as he continued the noises began again. Inexperienced as he was, he cut his visit a little short, went outside, and checked the car. There was nothing. Satan had won a victory!

Palmiro did eventually go to church with Dona Rosalina and accepted Jesus as his personal Savior. His faith brought about victory, which lasted as long as he resisted. Later, though, he changed back into the old person.

In fact, he was much more violent in his second state.

These things happened while Bobby and I were so young and inexperienced, but they helped us recognize that our fight is not against "flesh and blood," but against "the rulers of the darkness of this world, against spiritual wickedness in high places" (Ephesians 6:12).

※

Rosária came into the meeting hall when a service was in progress. She had entered because she liked the music she heard. She began attending and accepted Christ as her Savior.

Then she began working in our home. Often she told me of her experiences with Spiritism, even though she had never been a practicing spiritist. She told us of how some years earlier the spiritists she knew wanted to get her involved in Spiritism. Someone slipped a piece of her clothing from her house and took it to the spiritist center. After that, she began having a terrible headache. The headache was very strange. It covered only one side of her head and was an excruciating pain. Doctors could not find the problem. That went on for a while with no relief.

Rosária's friends said she could find healing by attending a spiritist session, but she did not succumb to their efforts to convince her to go. Then one day a spiritist friend told her that she could have the headache removed. She took an article of Rosária's clothing to the center. Even before the friend got home, the headache was gone never to return.

Satanic power brought about the headache to convince Rosária to get involved in Spiritism but, after that did not work, the cure came about in order to convince her that Spiritism is good. Satan works in strange ways!

※

A very dear person started attending First Free Will Baptist Church in Ribeirão Preto. She came because she was perturbed by the death of a niece, who had thrown herself from the window of her eighth-floor apartment. The woman accepted Jesus Christ as her personal Savior and seemed to be growing in the Lord. Each time Bobby and I visited her there were two things that dominated her conversation. First, she always talked about her niece; and then she would give us information about the way her husband was so against her decision to follow Jesus and attend church services. It seemed the pressure was building up between her and her husband. Bobby and I gave the best counsel we knew how to give. We prayed with her and for her.

Then one day we received a phone call giving us information about the woman's death. She had left home, as if everything was normal. She went out to the river just outside of town, left her identification, jewelry, watch, and outer garments stacked neatly there beside the river. Then she jumped in the river, committing suicide. Is it possible that the demon of suicide, which caused her niece to jump from her apartment, had entered her as well?

The young woman needed help. She worked in the offices at a large university. During the day, she seemed to be normal, always able to do her work. When she reached home at night, she became a different person. Much of the time, she seemed to be in a trance and knew nothing that she was doing. Some strange force was controlling her. Several times Bobby and I visited her and her husband. We had prayer with them and even dealt with the demons.

After each visit, she seemed to make improvement. Finally she agreed to go to church for a special service. I decided to sit beside her. I wanted her to feel welcome, and I wanted to be aware if any demon activity was going on. Things seemed to be going well. She was paying attention to the message when all of a sudden she completely changed and started mumbling unintelligible things. I called Bobby's attention to the situation. He and the deacons took her out and dealt with the demons. She seemed to have victory, but she would not go back to church and did not want any more help, thus all track of her was lost. The outcome is unknown to us.

A number of the men missionaries gathered in Pirassununga to help in a citywide evangelistic campaign. The campaign was going well and the night services were a blessing. People were accepting Jesus as their personal Savior.

About the middle of the week, the devil really "got riled up" and turned over a large cabinet onto the floor in the kitchen. At the same time, the girl working in the home went into a trance. The missionaries started dealing with her, asking God to free her of the demons. She went into a rage. It took the four men present to be able to hold her down. As they prayed, she would try to free herself even by biting the hands of the ones holding her down. She kept repeating in a deep guttural voice, "I hate Jesus. I hate Jesus. I hate Jesus." As the missionaries dealt with the demons, they asked them to identify themselves. They responded with something that let the missionaries know there were many of them. The demons kept saying, "She is mine. She is mine. Leave her alone." They tried to deceive the missionaries as well by saying that they were leaving, at which time the victim would calm down; but as soon as the missionaries relaxed their hold on the girl, she would start all over again.

This kind of ministry is certainly strength sapping, and victory only comes after many battles and through much prayer. The redemptive grace and power of God can do great things for those who resist satanic power.

§§

Just recently during my Prison Epistle's class at the Bible College held in the First Free Will Baptist Church in Ribeirão Preto, the receptionist came to the door. She asked to see her dad who was in the class. He went to the door where his daughter and I were standing. They stepped outside into the hall. Immediately he turned and said, "I need to go home. Is that alright?" He left without getting any of his belongings. Jacqueline saw my concern and said, "Mom said Rafael is acting in a strange manner. She thinks he may be demon possessed." The students were taking a test, so I spent a few minutes thinking and praying about the situation. For some time I had felt that Rafael was not true to what he professed, perhaps faking a relationship with Christ.

Celso arrived home and confronted Rafael. The father was convinced that the CD's were demonic and the demons were influencing or controlling his son. Celso and Maria Helena prayed, rebuking demonic power over Rafael. Celso, along with Rafael and his mother, took the CD's, broke them, and burned them. They were looking at the fire. Suddenly Rafael gazing at the fire said, "The CD's can't be demonic because there is a person dressed in white walking around in the fire." His dad told him that the one in white was the devil's way of deceiving him and for him to check the fire again. He looked the second time. That time the image in the fire was a hideous creature dressed in black and red. Rafael was shocked. Celso asked his son if he had really accepted Jesus as his personal Savior. He said he had not, but he wanted to. After he prayed, asking forgiveness for his sins, his countenance completely changed. According to his dad, he was a different person.

Just because a fourteen-year-old boy's parents are Christians does not inoculate him from satanic attacks. Thank God, Rafael had a father and mother who are concerned about the spiritual well-being of their children and had the spiritual insight to deal with the problem.

Bobby wrote in September, 1992: "I remember thinking when we first heard about AIDS that we would not be faced with that problem for a long time. However, it has not been that long. Within the past ten days, we have had funerals for two young men, both AIDS victims!"

Just because a young person is active in a church does not inoculate him from the possibility of becoming a drug addict or becoming HIV positive. Pressures are so great until it takes a strong Christian to resist. We have had those who were faithful in Sunday school and in youth meetings turn to the world, then later become HIV positive and even develop AIDS. The positive thing is, when they get the disease they return home where they can receive help. That is when the pastor/missionary has the opportunity of presenting the love of Christ and helping the person to make things right with God.

One day a friend asked Bobby to visit a young man in the Clinic Hospital. The young man had been part of our youth group when he was a teenager. When Bobby found him, he was on a bed in the hallway. During the visit, the patient became nauseous. Bobby did all he could to help him. He could not control himself so when he vomited, the secretion went all over Bobby's hands and some on his face. When Bobby came home, he told me that if he got AIDS it was because of that hospital visit. But God protected Bobby. During one of Bobby's visits, that young man repented of his sins and came back to the Lord. It was just a short time after that day of repentance that he was gone from this world.

Another young person came to know the Lord through the ministry of one of our sons in the faith. A new convert wanted to study in our Bible College in the First Church. Before he was converted, he was a drug user who got the HIV virus through injection of drugs. He had tested HIV positive, thus, he wanted Bobby to know about that before he started studying. He believed God had a plan for his life. He became active in the work of the Lord. He worked with the music, made visits, cut grass, gave Bible studies, and in short, he was the kind of Christian any pastor would like to have in his church. Everyone admired his faith and love for the Lord. Then one day he became very sick and, in less than a month, he went to meet his Master whom he had served so faithfully for a few years.

Another young man that we had known and worked with for a number of years, during his teen years, left home and started "living." The result was the HIV virus, which led to AIDS. We are so thankful that he made things right with God and gave a clear testimony of his faith in the Lord Jesus before he went to meet the Lord.

08.
FAMILY

"As for me and my house, we will serve the Lord." JOSHUA 24:15

Bobby and I arrived in Brazil after being married only three months. Bobby has often told people that he and I arrived in Brazil for a long extended South American honeymoon. After becoming husband and wife, we traveled the three months we had before our departure date, so we did not set up housekeeping until arriving in Brazil. Brazil brought about new experiences. I learned to cook using what we could find in Brazil. Just recently, an overseas apprentice said, "Brazil has the best food in the world." Dr. Robert Picirilli once said that he had never eaten better food than in Brazil. There is an abundance of food in the area where we live. During the Second World War, many Japanese came into Brazil and became the truck farmers; thus, there is an abundance of fresh vegetables and fruits. Brazil is a great cattle country, so beef is inexpensive. In fact, chicken has been much more expensive than beef. One of the blessings of living in Brazil is the affordability of filet mignon.

In those early days the Brazilian often said, "You don't have any children. Don't you want children?" Bobby and I soon realized that children could be a blessing as far as the work was concerned. We also knew that our family would not be complete without children. Robert Craig Poole was born on November 18, 1962.

Even before the conception of a child, Bobby and I had often prayed that God would give us children that would serve the Lord. We did not want to bring children into the world that would not love and serve the Lord

Jesus. Nor could I bear to think of a child born into our family spending eternity in hell.

Before time to leave home for Sunday school on November 18, 1962, the birth pains had already started, but I was not sure because I had had contractions throughout the whole pregnancy. There was no one to teach my Sunday school class so I did the teaching. When we met for the closing exercise, I asked Bobby to close out quickly because I needed to go home.

By the time we got home, the pains were every five minutes with durations of about a minute. It was time to call the doctor. The doctor told us to meet him at the hospital at 1:00 p. m. The baby made his appearance shortly after 3:00 p. m.

Bobby had already made plans with the doctor to be in the delivery room during the birth. It was comforting for me to have him there beside me during that important time. A medical school student that we knew quite well was also there. He asked Bobby to write a telegram so he could go to the post office and send it to my parents. Only the next day when the mail ran did they get the message "Robert Craig arrived safely. Mother and baby are doing fine."

When we arrived in Brazil communications except by mail hardly existed. The telephone system was very poor, taking eleven hours or so to get a call though to the U.S. The mail system did not have streamline speed as well. It took from ten days to two weeks for an airmail letter to arrive from the states. Even though we lived so far away and communications were so poor, we wanted our family, especially the grandparents, to feel a part of the growing up of their grandchildren. We tried to keep our parents aware of their activities. I would like to share with you parts of the letter I wrote on January 20, 1964, to my parents not long after their first grandchild turned one year old.

Dear Grandmother and Granddaddy,
I look at your picture and wish it were you in person so you would be able to talk and play with me. When we go home to the states, I'll be

big enough to help you (at least get in your way). My mommy says the only way I help her now is I keep the house in a big mess. She does not mind too much though, for she tells me I am more of a joy than a hindrance.

I am a little explorer. The other day I noticed that Mother was busy and not watching me, so I opened the gate and went out to explore the sidewalk, and soon would have explored the street, but a neighbor saw me and was taking me home when Mom noticed I was gone and went to search.

I like to imitate what Daddy does. One day when we were riding in the car, Mommy said something and Daddy teasing her reached over, slipped her skirt above her knee, and slapped her on the leg. Well, I did likewise. If I see Daddy kiss Mommy, I don't miss the opportunity to kiss her, too. Sometimes when Mommy is reading a book, I get one of my books and jabber about the pictures. Jklmnbgyfrjkl,.; I doubt if you understand my typing. Well, it says that I love you very much.

Your grandson,
RoberT

Young and full of adventure, Bobby and I, along with Robert who was twenty-one months old and missionary Mary Ellen Rice, decided to make a several thousand-mile trip down to the border of Uruguay. At that time the Fulchers, the Robinsons, and Molly Barker all worked in Riviera, Uruguay.

We decided on the interior route, which would allow us to visit friends along the way and to visit the famous Iguaçu Falls as well.

We left the hot interior town of Ribeirão Preto with temperatures above 90°. Two days later, we were in Cascavel (Rattlesnake), Paraná, which had sub-freezing temperatures. That night is the only time in Brazil that I remember waking up with ice in a glass of water on the bedside table.

After leaving the state of São Paulo, there were few paved roads. Our first tourist stop was Iguaçu Falls. In 1964, the falls had not become so popular. We spent a relaxing day out at the falls trying to see all of them and from as many directions as possible. The falls are on the Iguaçu River fourteen miles before it joins the Paraná River and forms part of the border between Brazil and Argentina. They are two hundred and thirty-seven feet high and stretch over an area two miles wide. At each bend in the trail, we would exclaim, "Nothing can be more beautiful," but many of the turns of the trail brought another even more amazing view. What a great way to spend our fourth wedding anniversary!

Leaving the falls we started south, but the rains had already started. The roads were slick as glass and almost impassable in some places. We made the trip in a jeep station wagon, which is a good vehicle for the dirt roads; but on that first day, we encountered stretch after stretch of roads where the ruts were waist deep. Transport trucks had stopped on each side. Naturally, Bobby got out and talked with the drivers. They thought he was somewhat crazy to be in that part of the country during the rainy season without four-wheel drive on the jeep.

At each of these places, Bobby got out, with his cowboy boots on, walked across the rutted area to see how solid the elevated areas were. Each time he returned to the car he said, "We can make it if I can keep the car up on top." Bobby drove through while Mary Ellen and I prayed. After going through several of those there was no turning back, so we continued on, not knowing what lay ahead.

The second day after we left the falls we made very little progress. The eighty miles we covered that day were laborious ones. Even growing up in rural America, we had never seen roads so slick. At times it was impossible to keep the car on the road. One day, three different times we had to get the car out of the mire and back on the road. What an experience! Actually, we thought we were making the trip before the rainy season began.

The next day the rains lessened, but the windshield would not stay clean enough to see where we were going. Therefore, we had to stop and clean it, and then continue on the slow journey. That cleaning process we did repeatedly.

One day back in the middle of nowhere, we ran out of drinking water. We found a place we thought would have bottled water, but they did not. They only had tonic water. Bobby and I had never had any experience with tonic water, but purchased some anyway. Since it came in returnable bottles, which cost more than the water itself, we emptied several bottles in a Tupperware container.

Back on the road again bumping along the rough road, we heard a puff sound and discovered that the lid of the water container had come off. I put it back on and a few minutes later the same thing happened again. The next time it happened, we decided to taste the stuff. Not being acquainted with tonic water and even less with such a taste, we thought it best to get rid of that undesirable by allowing the ground to soak it up.

In the state of Santa Catarina, we stopped in a small town called São José de Cedro. We thought we were in the old Wild West. All the buildings were wooden structures. The sidewalks were also made of boards. The hotel looked like the Wild West, except it was a one-story building and had no saloon. There was only one street, and it went up the hill to the Catholic chapel. Upon opening the door to our room, we saw an iron bedstead. Lifting the edge of the thick comforter, we saw the open springs. On the table were a washbasin and a pitcher of water. Under the bed was the "chamber maid." I have thought often that it would be good to have a film of that experience.

On the seventh day we reached Uruguay. Our time in Uruguay was fascinating. Learning and visiting the works was a great experience and just being with the missionaries was great. After a little over a week, the return trip was inevitable. That time we chose the costal route, but even that route had more than three hundred miles of dirt roads before reaching the paved ones.

Coming over the ridge we could see Ribeirão Preto in the distance. How good it felt to be back home, and how ready we were to get back to work.

Bobby and I had traveled in all the southern states of Brazil, but had never gone any further north than Rio de Janeiro. When our boys, Robert and John, were eight and five years old, we decided to go on another one of our adventures, a trip to the state of Bahia.

The main reason we chose Bahia was to check on a person with whom we had had contact through a home Bible study course, and who had a group of Christians meeting in his home.

It took three days to reach the small village where his family lived. Getting into the state of Bahia, we soon left paved roads behind. There were no road signs, no maps, and almost nothing to eat.

In one small village, Bobby stopped to ask directions. The young man said he would show us the way since he needed to go to the next town. He opened the door and climbed in. As many men during that time, he carried a small pouch which he kept on his lap. I did not know what was in it, so I kept my eye on it. The rider went with us to the next town and then gave us instructions to the next one. We continued on our way. After traveling all day, we finally got to Rio das Contas and found our way out to the village, Marcolino Moura, where the family lived.

We received the royal treatment. One of the first things we were asked was, "Would you like to bathe your feet?" We felt as if we had been transported back into the times when Jesus walked on this earth. Washing feet was a custom in that arid area because the people wore sandals and walked everywhere they went.

The family insisted that we stay for the evening meal. Since we were so far away from anything that resembled a restaurant, we accepted the invitation. Also, we knew that they would have been offended if we had not.

The women busied themselves with the task of preparing the meal. One person got some shelled corn, put it into the "pilão" and began pounding it to make the meal for the bread; another caught a chicken and proceeded to dress it; and yet another went down to the river with a five-gallon can. Naturally, Robert and John wanted to see the river, so the boys and I went along. When Esmeralda got to the river she walked out a little ways, filled her can with water (that was not crystal-clear), put the five-gallon can of water on her head and started walking. She casually walked home without even holding onto the can. The boys were surprised. "Look, no hands!" was what we all wanted to exclaim.

Getting back to the house, I thought it was wise to ask Bobby what he thought about going back the eighteen kilometers (eleven miles) to the nearest store to get some drinks or bottled water. Bobby thought it best. We certainly did not want anyone to get sick out this far from the kind of civilization to which we were accustomed.

The interesting thing about those drinks is that no one in the family had ever tasted a soft drink and had to be convinced that Bobby had not brought in strong drinks. We realized that we were in a place where the people had never seen ice, ice cream, a paved road, and many other things common in the state of São Paulo.

Esmeralda kept talking about my dress and about how pretty it was. It was a well-worn dress, so the next morning I gave it to her and said, "If you do not mind washing this dress you may have it." She became my shadow. When I powdered my nose, she got her puff and helped herself to some of my powder.

After the meal and darkness came, people began to gather in the living room of the small house. There was a bench and a few chairs, a table and an oil lamp. As soon as the room was full, they started the service. Naturally, they invited Bobby to bring a Bible study.

The family made sleeping arrangements for the missionary family. Bobby and I received the best bed, which was a little wider than a twin bed with a mattress two inches thick filled with rice husk. We were grateful for a place to sleep, but did have some inconveniences, such as the spaces between the slats under the thin mattress and the grunting of the pigs on the other side of the wall.

The next morning, as we prepared to leave, people began to gather. Bobby found out later that they had come with the desire that he baptize them. Our apparent haste to get things ready to leave gave them the impression that we were in a big hurry, so they would not ask him. We were saddened when we found out. O what a joy it would have been to stay a little longer for a baptismal service!

On that trip, we learned of so many needs. There was no school in the village, drinking water was inadequate, no churches or pastors, but there were a few believers. We still hold dear to our hearts that village in the interior of Bahia and those people. Often we have prayed for that family and have thought about going there to work.

For an attendance promotion at Sunday school, it was announced that on a particular Sunday, friends were to bring friends and the person who brought the most visitors would get a Bible. Robert was less than three years old so Bobby and I unintentionally left him out. One day during that week, Robert was playing in the yard. I heard him talking to someone, so I went out to check on him. It was a person who lived on our street. I paused to pay attention to what he was saying. To my surprise, he was giving a verbal invitation to come to our church on Sunday. I helped him a little by giving an explanation that the Sunday school was having a special attendance drive, and it would be a pleasure to see her in church on Sunday. Robert brought up the Bible, so I explained that the person who had brought the most visitors on Sunday would receive a Bible.

Robert gave out that kind of invitation several times during that week. Then one afternoon I took Robert with me on a number of visits, inviting people to go to church on Sunday. I had done this many times with little results.

At the end of Sunday school came the time to take the count. Robert, with my help, had been responsible for eighteen people present on that Sunday. His little face lit up with joy when he was asked to go to the front to receive his Bible.

Robert kept asking us to get him a little brother. Just before his third birthday, his wishes became a reality with the birth of his brother, John Dudley. At first, Robert seemed puzzled and did not know what to do. He was encouraged to hold his hand and put a kiss on his forehead, and even allowed to sit with John in his arms. Then one day Robert's frustration was put into words: "John can't talk, can't walk, can't play. He can't do anything." As John began to notice things about him, he very much enjoyed Robert paying attention to him. They were soon giggling together and enjoying each other.

John had been born just two months before our family went to the U.S. for our first furlough. God gave us a very good baby. In fact, he slept eight hours the first night he was home from the hospital. That schedule continued, so he did not require night feedings.

Robert took on the responsibility of looking out for his little brother. That lasted until they both married and were separated by a few thousand miles—with one living in the states and the other in Brazil.

§§

It is good for children to have grandparents, especially grandmothers. Robert and John had two precious women in Brazil that they called Vovó (grandmother) Isabel and Vovó Tereza. Vovó Tereza lived in Albertina, a farm village, so contacts with her were less. Vovó Isabel lived just a few blocks away and attended our church, so contacts with her were many more. They loved and treated those ladies as their grandmothers away from home, and the women loved them and treated them as their own grandchildren. In fact, Vovó Isabel let it be known that our two boys were just as much her grandchildren as her own blood ones were. She told them stories, taught them Brazilian silly rhymes, put wet salt (her medicine) on any place they hurt, prayed for them, and loved them.

Both of those dear ladies went to be with the Lord within a year's time of each other, during the time that Robert and John were in the states for college. Bobby and I visited each of them not long before they died. Vovó

Tereza was in the hospital about forty miles away. Her children had said she would not recognize us because she no longer knew her own children. We quietly went into the room. She had her eyes closed. Bobby leaned over her bed and softly asked, "Vovó Tereza. Are you hearing me?" She opened her eyes and said, "Pastor Bobby." Then she looked at me and said, "Dona Geni." She never left the hospital. What a precious saint of God that humble woman was.

Vovó Isabel had gone to Campinas to live with one of her daughters. Bobby and I had contact with her mostly by phone; but one day we made the three-and-a-half hour trip to see Vovó Isabel. The same thing happened there. We were told that she would not recognize us, but she did and called us by name. Could it be that being the instruments God used to help these precious women in their walk with the Lord, we made such an indelible impression upon them that they remembered us even in the face of death? Thank God, they were a part of our lives and we had been a part of theirs. God brings people together who are of kindred hearts.

God brought to us another person that the missionary family in later years called "Bisa" which was short for "bisavó" (great grandmother). She is the great grandmother of our grandchildren who live in Brazil.

She moved three houses down from the church and started taking her grandchildren to church. She was as faithful as clockwork and was also a prayer warrior. For a number of years before her death she was completely blind. She would remember her missionary pastor's family by slipping into my hand some money to buy the boys ice cream. As the years passed, John married one of her granddaughters. He later became her pastor. She always loved and respected our family, so she remembered us even after almost everything else had faded from her memory.

I recall the testimony she gave in the church a few years after she had become a church member. At that time, we were studying Proverbs during prayer meeting. The verses about alcoholic beverages were covered. The Holy Spirit worked. One night during prayer meeting, Dona Zoraide stood up and spoke. She told us that ever since she could remember, she had taken a shot of wine after the meal to help with digestion. That was her family tradition even back in Italy. She said that Renata, her granddaughter, kept telling her that she should not do that since Christians did not partake in alcoholic beverages. She had never paid any attention to Renata, but the Word of God brought conviction to her that she should stop. She gave her testimony that night that the habit was in the past.

It was a joy to hear that dear person pray. When she prayed she really was on holy ground with God. We are so thankful to have known her and to have become an intricate part of her life.

§§

The first stateside assignment was a welcomed time. We would be with our families and the children would be able to enjoy their cousins. We had many miles to travel so we made preparations for the comfort and well-being of our three-year-old and two-month–old sons. They both needed their own beds, so we obtained a portable crib and a folding cot, which became a part of our luggage for the forty thousand miles we traveled during that year. God supplied a car large enough to take care of the needs of the family—an LTD Ford.

I have often admitted that not having the security of a home during that year did take a toll on the family. Robert's disposition helped him to survive the many miles of travel. He had the backseat as his haven and spent the hours playing. John needed more space and did not do so well. His bed was a pillow between Bobby and me. As the months went by, he wanted to be free. Needing freedom caused him to become frustrated and more irritable on our trip to California. On the return trip to South Carolina, I noticed he had a little fever. His nervous system was out of balance, which caused him to have a convulsion.

Robert immediately knew something was seriously wrong. He said, "What can I do, Mom. Do you want me to pray?"

Bob speeded up to a hundred miles an hour hoping a police car would appear, but it did not. Those were long miles into the city of Flagstaff, New

Mexico. By the time we got to the hospital, John was better. After a doctor examined him, he advised us to go to a hotel for a night's observation before traveling again.

That first stateside assignment finally ended. After a lovely visit with our families at Christmas time, we made our way back to our adopted country.

After that first stateside assignment, we went back to language school for a one-semester refresher course. In order to take the course, we rented a house in Campinas. Bobby attended classes in the morning and I in the afternoon. The boys were enjoying being at home and playing together with G.I. Joe and all his equipment. For John, that was a new experience since he had traveled most of his life.

While Bobby was at school, I began receiving anonymous, obscene phone calls. The caller spoke in rather broken English, and I spoke only in Portuguese. That went on for quite some days. In fact, Bobby and I began answering the phone using John 3:16 or other appropriate Scripture verses. The person on the other end of the phone line would utter a few curse words then disconnect. Evidently he knew more profanity in English than anything else.

During that time, Holiday on Ice was in São Paulo, which was just a little over an hour away by bus. Bobby and I had never seen such a performance, so we arranged for our Go-Ye Fellowship missionary friends, Uncle Frank and Aunt Katherine, to stay with the boys while we enjoyed an evening out.

Never before had the anonymous caller telephoned at night. But that night he did. His threat came loud and clear, "For the good of your children, you had better get out of Brazil." Naturally, that upset Uncle Frank and Aunt Katherine.

The next day Bobby went to the phone company to put in a complaint and ask for the number of the incoming phone calls. They could not or would not cooperate.

The threats continued, most of the time when Bobby was not at home. Finally, one day Bobby happened to be at home and answered the phone. He showed strength and courage in talking to the coward. In fact, that is one thing he called him. Bobby also told him that he did not believe he was going to do anything, but he was simply trying to make our lives miserable through his uncouth prank. He also said that if we got one more phone call, he was going to the police. Bobby told him that he had better be careful since what he was doing was against servants of God. Then he told him that God loved him and gave His life for his salvation.

That was the end of that unforgettable episode.

One morning Bobby walked out the front door. He saw something strange lying on the grass. It was a small package covered in plastic. Immediately he recognized that it had something to do with a curse that a spiritist was trying to place upon our family, more than likely because we were faithful in giving out the truth about the Lord Jesus Christ.

Bobby came back into the house and showed me the package. Together we opened it. Among its contents were incense and money. What were we to do with these things? The first thing we did was to pray, asking God to take away any evil influence, to purify the money, and give victory over Satan. Then we discarded all the other things by putting them in the trash, and we spent the money to buy milk.

That incident reminded Bobby and me how great God is. God is able to cleanse, purify, and protect.

A small shopping area had been built across the street from our residence. In one of those little store spaces, a spiritist group opened a center (a meeting place). Each afternoon at a certain hour, the door was opened. A few people would gather for a spiritist session.

When I was home, I felt led by the Holy Spirit to resist the clutches of Satan upon those lives. I prayed. Then I would go to the piano and play the hymn, "What can wash away my sin, nothing but the blood of Jesus."

The blood of Jesus and spiritism do not mix. I am very thankful to God that, within a few weeks, there was no longer a spiritist center across the street. What a great thing God had done!

§§

Robert was in the second grade. He was enjoying going to school and was doing well. During the first parents' and teachers' meeting, I received the information that the students would be doing several posters that year. I questioned if the student had to do the assignment on his own, or if the parents could help him. I was given the answer that the parents should help their children.

Robert attended school in the afternoon session. Lunch was over and he was about ready to leave for school when he began to whine and say that he could not go to school—because he had not made the poster he needed to take.

I looked at my watch and noticed we had forty-five minutes. I said, "Hurry, and we will see what we can come up with. What is the subject?" After Robert answered, "Income taxes," I thought, *What does a second grader know about income taxes? What can we use?* Bobby had heard the conversation and grabbed a volume of the World Book Encyclopedia, which had an illustrated explanation of income taxes, which could easily be adapted to the Brazilian system.

After grabbing the one sheet of poster paper we had on hand, which by the way was black, I grabbed the construction paper and magic markers as well. We got busy to get a poster made. Quickly I drew off different colored moneybags to represent things like salary, deductions, net income, exemptions, taxable income, etc. while Robert wrote the words of what they represented. Bobby and Robert cut out the bags while I made red arrows that we placed from one thing to another, ending up with income taxes paid to the federal government.

Unbelievably, it turned out to be a colorful and attractive poster. At least it caught attention and was a simple illustration that made it easy to go through the process of income taxes.

Robert made it to school with his poster on time. Soon the poster was forgotten.

July was the winter break from school. Classes began again in August. Robert did not return to the Brazilian school because furlough time had come for our family. Just a few days before we were to leave for the States, we received a telephone call from the principal of the school. She asked if we could take Robert to the school to receive his prize for winning the statewide poster competition. Representatives from the Itaú Bank, the sponsors of the competition, were there from São Paulo to make the presentation. I quickly got Robert dressed and Bobby took him to the school.

The ceremony was simple. Robert received a set of children's books. He was proud of his books. There never were too many books around for him. He already had a love for reading.

After the presentation, he did not go to class because he was no longer in school. He and his dad were standing outside talking with the representatives from the bank. One of the men put his hand on Robert's head and said, "Robert, you surely did a good job on that poster." Robert quickly replied, "Don't thank me. Thank my Daddy. He did it all." Bobby said that, if there had been a crack in the concreted area where they were standing, he would have liked to crawl into it.

After the sermon Robert heard on the way home, evidently he learned his lesson about presenting the wrong idea and speaking at a time when he should be quiet. After that, if Robert was talking too much or about to say what he ought not to, all Bobby had to do was say "Don't thank me," and a silence fell.

§§

The Brazilian school where Robert and John studied had a lot of poster making. When Robert was in the fifth or sixth grade, he had to make a poster for Aviation Day to remember the inventor of the airplane. Well, that presented a problem for him. He had studied in his American school that the Wright brothers were the inventors, but in Brazilian schools Santos Dumont—a Brazilian—was given credit for the invention of the airplane.

He made an attractive poster by placing the world map in the middle. From the country of Brazil he put a post, and from the post he put a pennant on which he put all the information he wanted to give. He used something to this effect: Brazil, be proud of your inventor of the airplane.

After the judging of the posters, Robert's teacher told him that if he had not put "your inventor" he would have won, because to the Brazilians there is no other inventor besides Santos Dumont.

For the celebration in the States of one hundred years of aviation, Brazil was the only South American nation that did not send a representative.

※

During our second term we were not only involved in a construction project, but also in the responsibilities of the work in Ribeirão Preto. As part of our outreach ministry, we held services in a small town about an hour's distance from Ribeirão Preto. At first these services in Luiz Antonio were held on Saturday night, and sometime later changed to a Sunday afternoon Sunday school followed by a worship service.

Both John and Robert were small; Robert was six and John was three years old. During that time, I was responsible for the youth meeting at the church in Ribeirão Preto. One week John would go with me, and Robert would go with his daddy. The next week they changed places.

John had a good characteristic for one who is a leader; when he made up his mind and made a decision, he did not easily give in. On one particular night, he wanted to go with me, but it was Robert's turn. I talked to Robert to see if he would change with John. He did not want to, so that meant that John would be going with his daddy.

Before Bobby and John left, Robert and I went up to the church to get things ready for the youth meeting. We had a good meeting that night and, after I locked the building, we all went our separate directions.

When Robert and I arrived home, we found Bobby sitting in the living room, with his belt handy and John on his lap. It was evident that John had been crying for quite some time and that he had been difficult to handle.

When I got the chance I asked Bobby what had happened. He gave me the story. He said that John continued saying he wanted to stay with me and would not get into the station wagon. Naturally, Bobby did not accept his decision and put John in the vehicle, went around the car and got in himself. At the same time, John opened the door and jumped out. No coaxing would get him into the car. Once again, Bobby picked John up and put him in the car. By the time Bobby got in the car on the driver's side, John was out again. The next time he told John not to open the door again. John obeyed, but he rolled down the window and climbed out. At that moment, Bobby decided his son was more valuable than just having one more service. He spent the next hour and a half or so talking to John, punishing him, praying with him, and crying with him. A victory had been won.

I am sure Bobby preached one of his best sermons that night.

While in Brazil I home schooled our boys in English, even though they also attended Brazilian school. Each week, in English school, they had to write a composition. For schoolwork, John wrote the following composition about his dad.

SOMEONE I ADMIRE

I admire a lot of people but someone I really admire is my father.

I admire the way he does everything like playing baseball, taking us to do things. But the thing I admire the most is his preaching.

I like the way he preaches and the way he can tell you things about the Bible. I admire him as a missionary as he tells the people in Brazil in South America about the Lord Jesus Christ. But the most important thing is to save them.

There are more things I admire my father for, like his sportsmanship. When he loses or wins, he is still happy. If he is in a contest and gets first, or second, or last he still does not get mad.

I admire my father for all the things he does.

※

One of the first things made real to Bobby and me when we arrived in Brazil was the fact that we were the foreigners. We realized that the Brazilians did not ask us to come, and some were not overjoyed at our presence in their country. Even though they were friendly and polite, Bobby and I felt the Brazilians could care less if we just simply packed our bags and returned to the United States. In fact, in those days we saw written on walls all over town, "Yankees, go home." These were not directed at us personally, but to Americans in general.

The big question was how we were going to get the people to listen to the message we had to share with them.

We soon learned that Brazilians are fond of social activities. They will have a party at the drop of a hat. Most of the social events are filled with eating and sitting around talking.

As time went on and Bobby and I recognized that our friends enjoyed the American-Brazilian mixture of a meal, we began inviting small groups to our home for meals. Sitting around after a meal gave us the opportunity to speak with them about the true and living God.

※

Literally hundreds of times Brazilians have sat around our dining table for a home-cooked meal. I remember one night when Dr. Wagner, a scientist whom I was instructing in conversational English, along with his wife, was having the evening meal in our home. The conversation came around to the subject of religion. Dr. Wagner said that his parents never mentioned the subject of religion; therefore, he had never thought about the need for God.

The conversation that followed that night made some changes. A short time later Dr. Wagner, along with his family, went to the United States for a two-year research program. While living and studying in North Carolina, they sought out a Baptist church where they attended.

Upon returning to Brazil, they contacted Bobby and me, their old friends. Because of that contact, Dr. Wagner and his wife became interested in hosting a Bible study group in their home to examine the Gospel of John. Week after week Dr. Wagner showed increasing faith. From that group two other people began attending church. That all started with English classes that led to a meal together and a time to talk.

§

Out of curiosity, one day I asked Carla, one of my Sunday school students, how it was that she started attending church. She asked, "You don't remember?" After I assured her I did not, Carla said that it was because of a meal in our home. I had invited Shizue and Rebeca, who had come to Ribeirão Preto for college. They were visitors in my Sunday school class looking for a church home away from home. The invitation was to include friends, so they brought two friends. Carla, one of the friends, was so impressed with the warmth of our home that she decided she wanted to have more contact with us. Shizue and Rebecca were already Christians who made the Free Will Baptist church their church while in college. Carla began attending Sunday school and later accepted Christ as her Savior. Praise God!

§

All through the years, Bobby and I have used our home to reach out to all age groups. We turned our basement into a game room with soft drinks in the refrigerator and brownies or homemade cookies available. Often children and young people have used it, and they bring along their friends. In this way, the ice is broken and soon some of the friends find it easier to accept an invitation to attend church or to talk about the Lord.

It would be interesting to know how many there are in church today because of an initial contact in our home. Thank God that He gave us a place that we can use in such a way!

I especially remember one occasion when it was time for our family to return to the field. As always there were mixed emotions, but it was different that particular time.

During that stateside assignment, I had seen my dad go through two lung surgeries. He was still weak from his second surgery when it was time for us to return to Brazil. I felt my parents needed me at home, but at the same time both Bobby and I had peace that we should return to the field as scheduled.

I knew that God was able to take care of my parents without me, and God was so good to prove He would.

A few weeks after getting back to the field my mom wrote that she had defrosted the chest-type freezer they had at the time. The drain stopped up and neither she nor Dad could bend over the side far enough to open the drain. Their frustration did not last long however. A complete stranger came to the door. He was a university professor who was looking for Dad to ask him to make an estimate on a track of timber. He saw my parents's dilemma and came to their rescue, not leaving until he had helped clean the freezer and put the frozen goods back in. A few weeks later my parents decided to go to visit my sister and her family who lived in Virginia. At the time, Dad had a car and a small pickup truck as well. He liked to drive the pickup so they started out in it. A couple of hours away from home on an interstate highway a water hose on the truck burst, but Dad did not stop immediately. He wanted to make it to the next exit and a gas station. The pickup overheated and stopped. What were they to do? No one seemed interested in helping. The cars just kept buzzing by. I am sure they both silently asked God for help.

Then help finally came. A car pulled off the road. A nicely dressed young man got out and asked if there was a problem. He immediately took my dad into a town nearby to get a mechanic to check the pickup. Then he helped get a wrecker to tow the pickup to a garage in dad's hometown.

The young man asked my parents what they wanted to do. After deciding to return home, the nice man told them he would take them. He drove them back to their home. As they got out of his car, they invited the stranger, who no longer seemed a stranger, to go in for a while. He refused. And, to the amazement of everyone, he refused any monetary exchange for his time, trouble, and expenses as well.

Once again, God had proven to me that He would take care of my parents.

I have often wondered if that stranger was not an angel in man's clothing. I have mentally pictured at what distance he got away from my parents' home before he vanished.

Bobby and I had made plans for quite some time for our two sons and their families to be together for a while in Brazil. July of 2001 was the date decided upon and preparations were made to make the time together very meaningful. Robert and his family came in from the U.S. Everyone was so excited! The six grandchildren were together for the first time. The three who lived in the United States understood almost nothing in Portuguese. The three who lived in Brazil spoke Portuguese, but had a reasonable amount of exposure to the English language. One concern was the possibility of a communication problem. That proved an unnecessary concern, however, because in some way they seem to understand each other.

This family of twelve had never been together at Christmastime, so we planned a July Christmas celebration. We set up a Christmas tree in the living room and soon many gifts were under it. Our family had a delicious dinner with all the trimmings, the kind we would have eaten on Christmas day. We relived the events in our minds as the Christmas story was told. We were reminded that Christmas had to happen for Jesus to be able to die for the sins of the human race. Robert went to the piano and played Christmas carols and the family joined in singing. After opening gifts, we had a good time just enjoying each other.

The family was together for three weeks. Ten days of that time, we traveled together and had a great time. The joy of those days together will always remain with us. One day we went to Campinas to the amusement park, HopRide. On the way, we stopped at a filling station for a picnic lunch of fried chicken, pimento cheese sandwiches, and chips. We had a lot of fun and enjoyed most of the rides. Often Bobby, when on one of the rides along with our sons and grandchildren, wondered why he was there. Cheri and I did more watching than riding.

The next day, after our trip to the amusement park, we left for the Iguaçu Falls. Our family was traveling together for the first time. The first day we drove about three hundred miles and stopped for three nights and two days to visit the rock formations called Vila Velha. Our grandchildren had a great time climbing and playing on the rocks. For lunch, we took out our picnic fixings. The only problem was, there were many little animal visitors called "quatis," which are about the size of an opossum. Stephanie was making herself a sandwich from the last of the pimento cheese when one of the little animals came up behind her, jumped on the picnic table, snatched the container from her hand, and ran off. All that happened so quickly that no one could stop him or even retrieve the container. It frightened Stephanie, but everyone else had a good laugh.

The next day we visited the sinkholes in the area. These sinkholes are large—about a hundred feet in diameter and two hundred feet in depth. An elevator took us down to the water level. There was constant water coming out of the ground over the rocks and spraying down into the pool at the bottom.

After that, we went over to the lake that the water from these sinkholes feed. It was a beautiful lake.

The next day we were on our way to the Iguaçu Falls, which was about another three hundred miles. Since the roads are not dual lanes, needless to say, it was after dark when we arrived. The temperature was dropping and it was getting very cold. The next morning there was ice on the windshields of the cars.

The Iguaçu River forms part of the border between Brazil and Argentina.

On that river, fourteen miles above its union with the Paraná River, are the beautiful Iguaçu Falls. These falls are 237 feet high and over two miles wide. It took a full day to see the falls on both sides. The Brazilian side was visited one day and the Argentina side the next day. We also visited the point where the three countries—Brazil, Argentina, and Paraguay—meet.

When we went to the Argentina side of the falls, we decided to use the restrooms before we started the long trek to see the falls. After standing in a long line to make our rest stop, we were to gather back at one certain place. Everyone arrived except Sarah, our ten-year-old granddaughter. Almost in panic, we all ran around trying to locate Sarah, but no one could find her. I knew she had gone into the stall after me at the restroom. I decided to go back to the restroom to check, but the attendant said she had already left. The search continued. I decided to go back to the restroom again where I asked the attendant if I could go inside to see if she happened to be there. I went in and called at the stall where I had last seen Sarah. She answered, "Grandmama." How good it was to hear that word! Sarah had not been able to get the door open and did not know how to ask for help, so she just calmly waited.

That afternoon we visited the Itaipú dam on the Paraná River, which was very interesting. It is one of the largest hydroelectrical dams in the world. It has eighteen or more generators.

One day we drove into Paraguay just to be able to say we had visited there. The city was such a madhouse that we decided not to get out of our cars. We turned and made our way back across the bridge. Even at that, we were almost two hours getting in and out of Paraguay.

On that trip, we had our breakfast at the hotel, ate at a restaurant at noon, and had a snack in the hotel room at night. After that snack, we all sat around and played games. That reminded Bobby, Robert, John, and me of the times at my mom and dad's house at Christmastime some years before.

The time flew by and Robert's family went back to Atlanta, Georgia. The third night after they were home, the phone rang. It was Robert. He said that they were sitting there talking about their trip to Brazil. He said that everything was very positive. No one had any kind of complaint; and that things could not have gone better. It was perfect.

※

It is unbelievable how long it takes to get things done in Brazil and how complicated a simple task becomes. Bobby does all the standing in lines and waiting and seems to have the patience of Job.

He wrote in one of his newsletters that that particular day was one of those days! It should have been simple enough. He had everything the "Cartório" (place to register documents) requested to register the minutes of the church's last business meeting. He had two copies of everything, which included the announcement on the bulletin board about the business meeting. This announcement had to have a date and be signed by the president of the church, which in most cases is the pastor. There had to be a cover letter requesting the registration of the minutes signed by the president, a copy of the minutes, and a page with the signatures of members who were present at the meeting.

With these papers in hand, Bobby went to another "Cartório" to have the signatures on the cover page and minutes notarized. Nothing turned out like it was supposed to! The "Cartório" would not notarize the name of the secretary of the church, even though it was the same place we had used the year before. Bobby went home to get a copy of the last year's minutes. While at home he called the secretary and found out she had her name registered in yet another "Cartório." He went back downtown with all the papers in hand to the Fifth "Cartório" and registered his name there to avoid having to go to yet another "Cartório" to get his name notarized. With all these papers in hand, he drove to another part of the city to yet another "Cartório" to register the minutes. He hardly had anything right since he was using the list given to him from the year before. After looking over the papers presented to him, the young man said, "Oh, this will not do!" He pulled out a list, which was different from the one Bobby got at the same place the year before, and said, "This is what you have to have." Bobby could not believe his ears, and he told him so. More information was necessary to register the church minutes than to get married! Normally, Bobby does not say anything about the bureaucracy, but that day his cup overflowed. No, he did not "blow up," but he did let them know how he felt. A missionary has to adapt to things like that or he will not last in Brazil. I guess Bobby and I have done a good job adjusting; we are still in Brazil!

Is that mission work? Yes, it is part of the package. I asked Bobby why he did not let the secretary register the minutes. She would have had to do all that running around by public transportation or walking, and Bobby is sure she would have been more "fed up" than he was.

A dear friend in South Carolina wrote the following in response to a newsletter that told of the incident.

"Mr. Poole, I got your email, "fed up"; and, at first, I laughed out loud. It was nice to know someone besides me gripes about the government and just how many ways they can mess up people's lives. We have a country store about two miles down the road from us, and they have a table where a bunch of us sit around from time to time. Those of us there are quite certain that if the president, secretary of state, supreme court, senate, congress, etc. would just listen to us, the world's problems could be solved quite simply. However, it did surprise me a little to learn that a missionary, especially someone of your steadfast faith and optimism, and, it seems, the patience of Job, could become "fed up." That's when it hit me that Jesus must have become frustrated at times dealing with the scribes and the Pharisees as well. After all, He walked this earth as a human, and they were constantly on His heels. Isn't it funny how you read Scripture over and over until you can almost quote it, but some parts of it don't really occur to you until something in your life coincides with it? I, too, like everyone, have griped about the "red tape" of government, and I have poured over the debates of Christ and the scribes and the Pharisees. Until I heard a man of your stature complain, however, I never thought about Jesus becoming frustrated or "fed up" dealing with all of it. Thank you, Bobby Poole.

Your not so saintly friend but still hangin' in, Ginger."

09.
A DECADE OF EXPERIENCES

"This sickness is not unto death, but for the glory of God, that the Son of God might be glorified thereby." JOHN 11:4

My brother-in-law, a medical professional, told me some years ago that each decade brings differences in a person's body; therefore, I should be prepared for change. One thing I did not realize was the drastic changes that can come into the life of a person.

All of these many years in Brazil, Bobby and I have tried to practice giving the Lord first place by worshipping, trusting, thanking and serving Him with all our heart. Nonetheless, there are times and events that have taken place in our lives which we did not understand; but we still knew that God was in control. There are things that made us want to cry out to God, "Why? Why is this happening to me?" Those thoughts brought Romans 8:28 to mind: "We know that all things work together for good to them that love God."

When speaking on this verse Bobby asks, "What are the two most important words in this verse?" After several responses such as love, all things, and purpose, he will say that the first two words, "We know," are the most important. If a person does not *know* that this verse is true, then he will go into a tailspin in cases like bad illnesses.

That "different" decade started during our stateside assignment in 1997. It started a chain of events, which at the time of this writing has lasted more than a decade. I would like to share these experiences with you since God has used this decade to draw both Bobby and me closer to our Creator and Lord, and has given us opportunities to be a witness to those whom we otherwise would have never met.

Our stateside assignment had taken us to several states and many churches where we shared with our people reports of the work in Brazil, and did a number of chalk drawings showing the need of pouring out Christ on a dying world. Each time we had a few days free from services, we would go to Bobby's homeplace in Tennessee to have as much time as possible with his elderly mother, Mama Poole. One of those times in Tennessee, our drama began.

Flea bites (yes, flea bites!) must have been the cause of the itchy spots on my arms. I did not think much about the spots since there were dogs around, and if a flea is anywhere nearby, it seems to be able to find me. The allergy cream should have taken care of the spots, but applying it did not help. Within a couple of days blisters had formed. Other spots and blister came. When the blisters burst, there was sensation as if it were a fire burn. The suffering became more intense as they spread to my hands, neck, and then feet. I was up most of the night trying things to bring relief so I could get a little sleep. Even in the cold winter I could not cuddle up under the covers; in fact, I could not even bare to have a sheet over me.

Bobby and I were not in one place long enough to find a doctor until we were with Rev. Bronco and Mozel West in Dunn, N.C. Mozel set up an appointment for me with the dermatologist she was using. The doctor was honest and said he did not know the cause, but it could be mites since we had recently visited a zoo. The mite treatment did not help.

Our next stop was Florence, S.C. Because of my misery, I asked Bobby and a cousin of mine to take me to the emergency room at McLeod Hospital. The first disagreeable thing I encountered was the comment of the receptionist, "Are you sure you want to be checked here? You know it will cost you $300." I had already called a number of dermatologists in Florence, failing to get an appointment. Actually I wanted to scream, "If I could get a doctor I would not be here"; but I did not succumb to that desire, so I politely answered, "I am sure."

The doctor on duty that day said there were two kinds of mites, so he gave me another treatment. He also told me that I did not need to come back to the emergency room. After explaining that I did not live in the U.S. and I had called several doctors trying to set up an appointment, I begged him to refer me to a dermatologist, but he refused.

I was very disappointed in what I had heard from the doctor and his little interest in my case, evidently passing it off as nothing important. I went out into the waiting room and told Bobby, "He told me not to come back to the emergency room," then I burst into tears. Bobby asked to speak with the head of the emergency room and told her how I was treated. She asked us to wait so we could talk with the doctor. He admitted that he told me not to come back, that I did not need the emergency room, and that he would not refer me to a dermatologist. Nothing was resolved that day.

A man in Faith Free Will Baptist Church in Darlington, S.C., heard about the episode. He became involved because of my emergency room treatment. After returning to Brazil, a letter came from the hospital asking forgiveness for the way things had happened during my visit, and asking me not to allow the incident to keep me from using the hospital.

A day or two after the emergency room visit, Bobby and I received an invitation to a senior citizens' meeting at Sand Hill Free Will Baptist Church. Pastor Sherwood Lee, who is a friend (and at the time was a mission board member), saw my condition; thus, he set up an appointment with Dr. Welch at Olanta, S.C. After checking me, Dr. Welch said she thought the disease was in the Lupus family. She gave me a twenty-one day cortisone treatment, which brought the symptoms under control for a short time.

Soon we were back in Brazil. The medication had run its course. Blisters began to appear in my mouth. When the blisters burst, a burning raw sore place would result. My gums became red, swollen, and very painful. In fact, the gums were so swollen until my teeth felt like they would pop out. My regular dentist told me that she had never seen anything like what I had. She set up an appointment with a dental surgeon who took out one of the blisters for a pathologist to examine.

I will never forget the day I went back to his office for the results. I think on purpose He met Bobby and me at his office when no one else was there. He sat down on the couch beside me there in the waiting room and explained, "I wish I had good news, but I don't. The biopsy shows that you have pemphigus, which is an incurable disease." In Brazil, it is known as "fogo selvagem" (wild fire). It is more common in Brazil than in the States.

The dentist sent me to a dermatologist who was a specialist in that disease. He told me that all he could do was keep the disease under control since there is no cure for pemphigus. After trying several medications, which did not help, I began taking high dosages of cortisone. That treatment worked in controlling the disease, but there were side effects as well.

Either the disease or the treatment caused me to become very weak. The weakness played havoc with my mental state. I dropped into a depression that seemed to be sinking me. I felt that my time of usefulness was over. When Bobby was away from the house, I sat in my recliner and cried out to God, asking Him to take me on home to be with Him. I am so thankful that the depression lasted for only one week. My time of crying and praying brought me closer to God and I asked for His victory. God gave me a peace that passes all understanding and never again have I fallen into depression.

It was amazing how God worked! I did not miss teaching either my Bible College classes or the classes in the church. Each day when it was time for me to teach, my strength was renewed and I was able to teach. I praise God for that! He kept me active even in adverse circumstances.

At the end of the semester, several students gave testimony to the fact that I had been a blessing to them, as they watched me continue faithfully fulfilling my responsibilities of teaching even during that difficult time. Also I gave my testimony of how God did not answer the prayers I had sent up to Him, and how glad I was that He knew what was best for me. I was learning to depend on Him more and more.

After more than a year of high dosage of cortisone, the dermatologist began reducing the medication. It would take months to get me weaned off the medicine.

One Friday night while working at my computer, I felt as if my clothes were binding me on the left side. I examined the area where the pressure was. There was the lump. I showed it to Bobby, who said, "We will have to get that checked out," and continued with his work. Sometime during the weekend, I told Bobby that if he thought I needed to go to a doctor, I was going to leave it to him to set up the appointment. Early Monday morning he called the gynecologist's office and made an appointment for the next day.

Upon examination, the doctor said he thought it was nothing to be concerned about, but that it would need to be removed. He sent me to have a biopsy done.

Receiving the results and returning to the doctor, we learned that the lump was a malignant tumor. That was definitely news that we DID NOT WANT TO HEAR. My life was in danger, but God's peace ruled in our hearts. The gynecologist gave us several options: have the surgery by him, go to the U.S. to have it checked out, or have an oncologist in Brazil check it. We opted for a second opinion using a local oncologist that the gynecologist recommended.

We knew that God is all-powerful and can heal. He had healed me of polio when I was a child, and through that God had separated me for His work of missions. We asked our son John, pastor of the First Free Will Baptist Church, to bring some of his deacons over to Marincek Church. We wanted them to anoint me and pray for God's healing upon my body, if He so chose and He could be glorified through the healing. We all wanted God's will and timing done in my life.

Later as I thought about the Marincek group of Christians, who do not have means to get good medical treatment, I felt that if God healed me, it could have had a negative effect on the people if they asked God for a healing and did not receive it. I am thankful we serve a God who knows best.

After being anointed with oil and being prayed for, I did not want to go into surgery without a second biopsy. The doctor was kind and sent me for the second biopsy. The result was malignancy, but a different kind of cancer was determined. I was puzzled, but that confirmed that God's way of healing was to go though the medical process of getting rid of cancer.

The emails and phone calls came in by the dozens. Most of the calls gave us an assurance that the people were concerned and they were praying. There was one person in particular in Brazil who kept saying, "Believe, Geneva. If you have enough faith you will be healed." Bobby and I could not accept her reasoning. I knew that God was able to heal and that I did not lack faith, but more than anything else, I wanted God's perfect will to be done in my body and in my life.

I doubt that I will ever forget the day the oncologist told us that I needed surgery and "the sooner the better." He kept asking me how I was doing. I told him that I was fine, that my life was in God's hands, and that I had peace in my heart. That reaction was strange to the doctor because of the adverse reactions of so many whom he had already treated.

Bobby and I both were at peace in opting to have the surgery done in Brazil. God had placed us in the hands of the best. In fact, one doctor referred to Dr. Julião, the oncologist, as the pope of oncology in Brazil. He wanted to assist in the surgery, so the surgeon set the surgery for the Saturday between Good Friday and Easter Sunday, which is called Hallelujah Saturday in Brazil. He said that only emergency surgery can be set up for that day, but he considered mine an emergency.

Surgery went fine and I returned to my room in the early afternoon. I had been sleeping most of the day, but once in a while, I woke up long enough to know things were not exactly normal for the surgery I had. Between 3:00 and 4:00 that afternoon the surgeon came by. I asked him about the puffing in the area above the surgery. He told me that there was hemorrhaging, but it would take care of itself. I drifted off to sleep again, but soon woke up when it seemed as if something broke loose inside. Karen Cowart was sitting with me, so she called the nurse. My blood pressure had dropped and, a few minutes later, had dropped even more. I insisted that I needed my doctor. The nurse told me that I was just anxious and that everything was normal. I kept looking at my white hands and I knew things were not normal. The nurse heard my plea and called the doctor. He was still in the hospital and had me taken immediately back to the surgical unit.

Heavy blankets covered me as blood transfusions were started in the arm and in the foot. I did not want to lose consciousness, so as I was being stretched out in the form of a cross I said, "I thought yesterday was the day of the crucifixion." The surgeon came back with words that gave me peace. He said, "It was, but today is Hallelujah Saturday and we are going to have the victory." He began snipping stitches and said, "I hope it is not a generalized bleeding." I then drifted off into a peaceful sleep knowing that God would give the victory.

Things were made clear about the two different biopsy results on the next doctor's visit. The testing done during and after surgery showed that there were two tumors and each had a different kind of cancer cells. Approximately fifty lymph nodes had been removed. Exams showed cancerous cells in eight of them, which meant cancer was spreading and considered in the "third stage." As a result, I went through intensive treatments after surgery, which included six applications of chemo over a period of approximately four months, and thirty-five applications of radiation over a period of seven weeks.

The college semester break fell the week after surgery, which helped in our teaching responsibilities. The next week I was not able to return, but the third week I was back in the classroom. It was amazing to watch God at work, renewing my strength each time I needed it to be able to continue in the work.

We praise God for His care during what most people consider an ordeal! There were many opportunities to be a witness to people whom we otherwise would have never seen. A gift of a Bible and a testimony had an effect on a number of people. Among those who received a Bible from us was the oncologist. During one of our office visits, he said, "You think

I don't read the Bible you gave me, don't you? But I do." He opened it and read a verse from the passage that he had read that morning.

It is difficult to know why things happen the way they do. My theory (the oncologist agrees with me) is that the cancer possibly could have been a result of all the cortisone I had taken.

※

One thing led to another. The oncologist prescribed tamoxifen, a medicine to keep tumors from returning. Honestly, I did not want to take the medicine, but the oncologist thought it was necessary. I tried to obey, but missed about every third dose because of disinterest.

Soon my vision began to change. It was getting dimmer each day, so I called the oncologist, who did not think it was because of the medicine and assured me that I needed to continue taking it. After six weeks of taking tamoxifen, I went back to the surgeon. He asked me how I was doing. I responded, "Fine, except my vision is becoming more blurred each day." He asked, "You are taking tamoxifen, aren't you?" After my reply he quickly blurted out, "If you don't stop you will go completely blind." That was not a good thought. Bobby reached over and took my hand. I explained that Dr. Julião said it was necessary. He picked up the phone, called Dr. Julião and had the medicine suspended right then; but the damage had already been done. I was almost blind from the cataracts that had formed.

Sometime later Bobby and I went back to Dr. Julião for my routine check. He told us that he had gone to Europe for a medical convention. He was speaking twice, but had a break between his lectures. During that time, he attended a study on the effects of tamoxifen, and it is a proven fact that in less than two per cent of patients the vision is affected by that drug.

That led to eye surgery for lens implants. The surgeries were a week apart. I had been struggling to continue with my classes using a magnifying glass to read. Finally, the last Sunday school class I taught before the surgery Bobby did some reading to me.

The day I went for the first surgery, a woman a little older than me was also sitting in the waiting room. The process began there. A nurse came in and put drops in her eye and then in mine. I noticed from the few words spoken by the patient that she had a heavy accent, so I asked her if she was Brazilian. She said she was German and she and her husband had come to Brazil to work with the Antarctica drink bottling company. Her husband had already died; however, she decided to stay in Brazil. She then asked me if I was Brazilian. Upon hearing that I am an American she said, "In my next life I am going to be an American." I quickly responded, "Oh! I am not going to be an American. I am going to heaven where I will be with Jesus." She said that she wished she had that kind of certainty. I told her in the short time before she went out for surgery that she could have that certainty and quoted John 3:16 to her. The nurse came to take her out for surgery, so I told her to think about what God had done for her and encouraged her to begin studying the Bible, beginning with the gospel of John. I have often prayed for her, and I trust those words made an impression upon her life.

God was so good in giving me back my vision. More than ever, I want to use it for His glory.

While on the cortisone, several hot, feverish areas appeared on my legs, and the veins became very sensitive and hurt when touched. The dermatologist sent me to have the veins in my legs checked out. The doctor said I needed surgery, but he would not put a knife on me while I was taking the cortisone. Therefore, time passed. Cancer treatments were over, and I was no longer on cortisone. Then I returned to have the vein problem checked again.

The doctor sent me to have a vein scan done, which revealed that one vein in the upper part of my right leg was in a state of aneurism. The doctor did not want to wait. He wanted surgery immediately. Unless it was an absolute emergency, I did not feel that I could. Robert and his wife, Cheri, and their three children were coming to Brazil the next week to be with us for three weeks. We had planned to have Christmas in July and a ten-day trip with the whole family.

Hesitantly, he agreed to set the surgery for the second day after our son and his family returned to the States. Bobby and I depended on God's protection before, during, and after the surgery. Surgery went well and I have done great since.

During one of my checkups, the oncologist suggested that I was very much in need of taking an application of Zometa, a bisphosphonate, every six months to help my bones retain the calcium that could keep me from getting osteoporosis. Tests had shown that there was a definite reduction of calcium, so I agreed to the treatment.

I have always had problems with allergies, so I have often taken medicine to help with my breathing. During the stateside assignment in 2003, I began to feel that there was more wrong than just allergies. Each time I stooped over, my ability to breath became much more difficult. If I had to do anything to stoop over, I would sit down on the floor and work from there.

It seemed that when we returned to Brazil the problem was not quite so severe, so I let time pass without getting my allergies checked. But it was time for another application of Zometa. That time I asked that the doctor check my breathing before the application. He was not in the office that morning, but after a phone call, he gave the nurse permission to give the application. He gave her instructions to check several things, including the oxygen level in the blood. After more contact with the doctor, he asked her to keep me in the office until he could get there about 11:00.

Upon listening to my lungs, the doctor said there was a problem with fluid. He called the laboratory to ask them to make an x-ray immediately. By the time the x-ray was developed, he was there to see the results. He said, "You have liquid in the lungs, but the problem is with your heart." He allowed me to go home for an hour to get things ready to enter to the hospital. I was to return to the emergency room where he had already given instruction to start exams such as echocardiogram and blood tests and orders to admit me to the hospital. Unhappily, there was no room available, so there I stayed in the emergency room. The evening meal was served to both Bobby and me in the emergency room. About 7:00 that evening, I was admitted to the hospital. The heart specialist came by prescribing a number of medicines for me.

I thought that I was just gaining weight, but it was all body fluid accumulation. During the overnight stay in the hospital, medication eliminated fifteen pounds of fluid. How different my body looked. The next day I went home with a prescription for several kinds of medicine. My instructions were to return for an office visit in one month. After two weeks, I was feeling so bad that I called to set up an appointment. The doctor changed one medicine, dropped another, and gave me instruction to return in three months.

That was a long three months. I was feeling so lousy that I could hardly stand myself. The visits to my doctor were unsatisfactory. I did not know what to do. One day I called the oncologist and set up a regular appointment with him. On that visit, I talked to him about getting a second opinion. He said he would get in contact with me in a few days. He called after setting up an appointment for me with one of the professors at the University of São Paulo Medical School in Ribeirão Preto and in São Paulo as well.

During that first appointment with him he said, "We are not going to just treat symptoms; we need to find the cause." He sent me for another echocardiogram, which showed that the left side of my heart was in hibernation. Other tests did not give a reason for the condition, so I had a heart catheter to find the problem. It showed that one artery was blocked almost 90%. The test also showed that the problem was not from cholesterol plaque in the heart, which hardly existed, but from the growth of the lining of the artery. A week later, an angioplasty procedure was done to put a stent into the artery. How much different I felt after that! I was able to breathe and felt so much better. I kept active in the work. Bobby and I were thankful to God for the good results.

§§

After several applications of Zometa, I was having a problem with a tooth that was affecting my bite. Some years earlier I had lost the tooth beneath it; therefore, it had changed positions. My dentist recommended pulling it or doing an implant where I had lost the tooth. Since about 30 years had passed since I had lost that tooth, I decided to go the route of pulling the one that was affecting the bite.

Before the area had time to heal, the stitches pulled out. Going back to the dentist, she removed some spur-like pieces of bone and put in more stitches. That time the same thing happened again, leaving a bigger hole. My dentist could not understand what was happening, so she closed it up again. Once again, an even bigger place opened up. After that, she sent me to a dental surgeon to get his evaluation. His suggestion was that part of the bone needed to be removed, but he also suggested that the problem could be an immune system disorder.

Since I had used a dermatologist with Pemphigus, an immune system disease, I decided to check with him. About that time, a person in the Marincek Church mentioned my problem to her dentist whose cousin was a professor at the dental school of the University of São Paulo. He wanted to see me, so I went to him. His cousin was also present. These two dentists and the dermatologist agreed: Zometa had caused the problem, so the applications were suspended. The professor had just finished a post-doctorate course in the States; thus, he recognized the problem immediately, but had no solution about treatment. That particular problem was just beginning to appear here in Brazil. After both dentists did research, they decided that there was nothing to do except continuing to practice careful hygiene of the mouth. The exposed bone was a problem. Besides the normal hygiene, I went to my dentist several times a week for laser treatments. Each dentist I went to told me that I would have to have patience, because it might take as long as two years for the medication to leave the bone, allowing it to cover over with gum tissue once again. After about seven months, several pieces of bone came out. After that, the place began to fill in with gum tissue.

I was having a hard lesson in patience. I knew that God was in control. Through that ordeal, I wanted to be a testimony of God's grace. I constantly reminded myself that God's grace is sufficient.

About three months after the stent procedure in the heart, the original symptoms returned. I felt lousy—shortness of breath and a binding sensation in the chest area. The doctors decided on another angioplasty procedure, using the balloon instead of a stent. I went through that procedure, which gave some relief for only about twenty-four hours.

In less than a week, I was back in to see my doctor. I was not doing well, so he told me that day that it appeared nothing could be done except bypass surgery. He sent me that very afternoon to get another echocardiogram. The next morning, Bobby took the results of the exam to the doctor. A few hours later the receptionist called and set up an appointment for Bobby to go by and talk to the doctor. Our son John would not let him go alone, so they went together.

Bobby and John walked in the room where I was busy at my desk. John said that the news was not good. I smiled and replied, "I am happy." John replied that he did not understand how I could be happy "at a time like this." I gave a quick response, "I am happy because my life is in God's hands." I had never before felt a greater peace, that peace that passes all understanding.

On several occasions, Dr. Fernando had consulted with a colleague at the famous heart hospital, INCOR, in São Paulo, considered to be the best in Latin America. He wanted Bobby to take me to São Paulo for his colleague to examine me. He gave Bobby instruction to call Dr. Carlos on Sunday afternoon to find out the hour of the appointment in São Paulo for Monday. We were to be there at 12:00 noon on Monday. It was a five-hour trip from our home to the hospital.

My first impression of Dr. Carlos was what a kind, gentle, humble, soft-spoken person he was. He gave me a thorough exam, after which he gave his opinion. He said that it was our decision, but he felt I should not leave the hospital, and if no room was available that day, I should stay in the emergency room. He also said that I needed surgery as soon as possible. We were soon on our way to the admitting office. We were thankful they had a room and I entered the hospital.

After the stent was inserted, I had been taking a blood thinner. Because of the blood thinner, I could not have surgery as soon as originally planned. It should have been on Tuesday or Wednesday, but was finally done on Friday.

The surgery went well and so did the two days in the ICU. On Saturday, a week and a day after the surgery Bobby and me, along with our two sons, made the five-hour trip back to Ribeirão Preto. Robert had arrived in Brazil two days after my surgery. His presence was appreciated and a big help to Bobby. I feel so much better now than before the surgery. Walking for about an hour has now become a part of my daily routine.

On a routine visit, the assistant surgeon came by my room. I said, "I don't think we have talked before." He responded, "Oh, yes, we have. You don't remember it because of the medication, but you even laughed with me in the operating room. I was the one who held your heart in my hands during surgery. By the way, the muscles of your heart are in good condition. The problem with the artery was most certainly caused by the radiation treatments."

The days before going to São Paulo for the surgery, a phrase from the Psalms kept going over in my mind:"He shall give thee the desires of thine heart" found in Psalm 37:4. My desire was to be able to do much more for the Lord in Brazil, but most of all I wanted His perfect will done. I could not get away from the responsibility on my part to be able to receive this promise: "Trust in the Lord….Delight thyself also in the Lord….Commit thy way unto the Lord. . . . Rest in the Lord" (Psalm 37). I wanted to be Christlike.

I know that one day my heart is going to stop beating and that will bring an end to this life and earthly body, but not an end to the real person. This journey on earth is preparation for eternity with my Lord and Savior. Oh, how Bobby and I desire to help many more people make their preparations for eternity!

While at the hospital in São Paulo, Bobby and I had opportunities to speak to a number of people about the Lord and what He could do in their lives. In the ICU, one of the nurses came to me and asked, "You are a Christian, aren't you?" I was happy that evidently she had recognized something in me that showed her I was a Christian. Then I asked her, "Are you a Christian?" Her answer was positive. Another nurse came over to see if there was a problem. I asked her if she was a Christian. Because of her negative answer, I turned to the Christian nurse and said, "Tell her." What a blessed opportunity to be a witness!

I would like to share what the Lord taught me in the ICU. When I woke up, I had all kinds of tubes connected to me and I was on a ventilator as well. I tried to breathe on my own, but it did not work. I was breathing against the ventilator and I began to feel the lack of air getting into my lungs, then I realized what I was doing. I stopped trying to breathe and let the machine do it for me. Things worked well after that and I drifted off to sleep again. When I woke up, I did the very same thing again. It was then that God taught me a lesson. I began to think of how often I have wanted to take things into my own hands and not let God, the Holy Spirit, be in control. Life does not work too well like that.

§§

Some years ago, I went to a dentist for treatment of an abscessed tooth, which would require root-canal treatment. During all the sessions we thought he was cold, hard to strike up a conversation with, and very expensive as well. When my treatment was finished, we presented him and his assistant each with a Bible. We spoke with them about the love of Jesus, as well as what He has done for us.

Our paths did not cross again until a few years later when my dentist sent me back to him. He seemed so much friendlier that time. I was impressed. While talking to him, he asked, "Do you remember giving me a Bible?" He then filled us in on a little of what had happened to him since we had last seen each other. The very week that he received the Bible, his son invited him to go to a Bible study with him and a friend. He said he proudly got his newly received Bible that we had given him and went with his son. Soon he accepted the Lord as his Savior. Now he has a Bible study group in his own home with about twenty-five in attendance. He is a changed person and constantly speaks of the goodness of God to him.

But the story did not stop there. We have been able to take my regular dentist to the Bible study. What a blessing it was to have her sit beside me and read a verse when it came her turn and watch her as she listened intently to the words of the leader. The study was an excellent one. I am praying that we will soon see her active in the work of the Lord.

※

You may wonder how much mission work Bobby and I were able to do during this decade of sickness. There were times when activities slowed down somewhat, but most of our teaching and church responsibilities were fulfilled. Even during the semester of my heart surgery, I taught the first two months and Bobby took my classes after the surgery. I was still able to help him by correcting all the papers. Even after feeling stronger, I knew it would be difficult to teach three hours straight, and it would be unfair to the students to switch back and forth. The third Sunday after surgery, I was back in the Sunday school class, which in the Marincek church is an hour and fifteen-minute teaching period. The only time we were unable to fulfill our obligations were the two weeks in the hospital in São Paulo. I called the days before surgery a "forced vacation" that gave Bobby and me time together that we needed.

As far as I can tell the open doors to witness was an advantage; thus, an area of service to those in the medical field had been added.

§§

You may also wonder why we did not go to the States for all of my treatments. There were a number of reasons. We live in a part of Brazil where excellent medical treatment is available and, because of being Americans, we are sent to the most renown in their field. In fact, the heart surgeon could have been the one to do surgery on the president of the country if he needed it. Also, getting treatment in Brazil would not take us away from our mission work for months at the time. We also felt that it would be easier to stay in our own home and surroundings while going through the treatments. There was also an advantage financially. Costs are much less in Brazil than in the States.

One day during the time when we were deciding where to have the cancer surgery and treatments, our daughter-in-law came from across the street to see us. She broke down in tears and said, "I do not want you to go to the States." She and John did an excellent job in helping us during the decade of sicknesses.

§§

After the heart surgery, one night Bobby brought in a letter from one of my students in the Bible College. I would like to share it.

Dear Dona Geni,

I praise God for your life, because if it were not for you I would not have learned about Jesus. Thanks for all the classes in Sunday school; the Word planted in my heart gave me strength to come back to the Lord.

Your example as a missionary, wife, mother, etc., is always in my memory and your image helps me to be firm.

I am ever so grateful to God for the opportunity that He gave me to learn and put into practice the things learned from you and Pastor Bobby.

God was very merciful to give me the chance to have another opportunity to study under both of you.

Thanks for your silent example, which I only perceived and appreciated after many years. Your example was much greater than even your words.

Forgive me for not understanding you when I was teenager.

It is my heartfelt desire that God bless you and continue His work through you.

With Love, Cris

CONCLUSION

"Minister . . . as good stewards of the manifold grace of God."
1 PETER 4:10

When people ask Bobby or me how long we have been in Brazil, our usual response to a younger person's question is, "I think we discovered Brazil before you did," and then we tell them the number of years. One day a person responded, "Forty-five years—that is a lifetime!" My quick reply was, "I hope not. We want to be around a while longer."

I wrote shortly after our forty-sixth wedding anniversary: "When we came to Brazil in 1960 we had in our minds that we would spend all of our working years in Brazil. I remember saying to Bobby that, when we reach retirement age, we will have been in Brazil for forty years. That seemed like something that was so far off, why even think about it. Since the years roll by quickly, we are now in 2010. If God so chooses, this year we will celebrate our fiftieth wedding anniversary and our going to Brazil as well. Looking back, we feel the time has been too short. Oh, how we wish we had another life to live for Christ in this country. There is still much to do. As long as we have the health to continue to do the work that is required of a missionary, we plan to remain in our adopted country.

Many years ago, Bobby and I made a lifetime commitment to taking the gospel to the regions beyond. God called us to Brazil, and until He lets us know it is the time to go elsewhere we plan to continue in our adopted country serving our Lord and our denomination. Not even our son, daughter-in-law, and grandchildren in the States would have us to do otherwise. Our families have always backed our decision to work in Brazil.

Just recently, I received am invitation to give a chalk drawing in a church started by a graduate of our Free Will Baptist Bible College in Ribeirão Preto. At the end of the service a man of some fifty plus years, came up to me and began telling his story. He said, "You do not remember me, but I remember you. During the first years of your ministry, I went to your church with my grandfather. We moved away and found a church nearer to our house, but you, Pastor Bobby, and the God you serve made a lasting impression upon my life. My walk with God started under your ministry."

Bobby and I both say, "How thankful we are that God has worked through us down through the years and, once in a while, He gives us a boost when we learn of those we did not even know our lives had touched and influenced."

Our first love is for our Lord and Savior Jesus Christ. Our desire is that all we do, say, are, and have will be used for His glory. We count it a privilege to have had the opportunity to work as ambassadors for Christ, representatives of the Free Will Baptist denomination and laborers in His harvest field of Brazil. This experience of seeing people come to the Lord and get involved with the work has been a blessing that words cannot adequately express. Untold blessings have come to us, as we have remained faithful to the calling of God upon our lives. May God continue to work in Brazil.

For many years my favorite hymn has been "More About Jesus Would I Know," written by Eliza E Hewitt. It is interesting that the translation for "about" is "of" in Portuguese. A couple of good synonyms for "about" is "concerning" or "regarding," but "of" in Portuguese designates a relationship in which there is control. I want Jesus in control of my life.

As this hymn says or implies, I desire:
-To have more of Jesus in my life;
-To show more of His grace to others;
-To see more of His saving grace manifest in others;
-To have more of the love of Christ in me;

-To know more of His holy will; and

-To have the Holy Spirit teach me more of a life sold out to Christ.

Our son John has followed the example of his parents and ministers in Brazil. At present, he pastors the First Free Will Baptist Church in Ribeirão Preto, which according to information we have received is possibly the largest Free Will Baptist church on foreign soil. In 2008 he wrote the following article for *One* magazine.

I REMEMBER

THE WORDS "RENDER TO CEASAR THE THINGS THAT ARE CEASAR´S; AND TO GOD THE THINGS THAT ARE GOD´S" resound in my mind. I want to pay tribute to my parents, Bobby and Geneva Poole, who recently completed 48 years of non-stop missionary work in Brazil. I believe a tribute to someone compiles all a person is and has done, then acknowledges it all would have been impossible without God's intervention.

I admire you for leaving for a place totally unknown in December 1960, after only three months of marriage. You've stayed for a lifetime, never abandoning your post, serving faithfully throughout all these years. I salute you for your perseverance.

I appreciate your love for the Lord and for His harvest. I know your commitment is not only due to your obedience to your missionary calling; but also, because you experienced God's love, you want to share His love with those you minister among.

I am grateful for the vision you've had—starting new ministries in our church and town, where none previously existed. I remember when you worked hard to bring the Gideon's International to our city so Bibles could be distributed in our region. I remember you beginning the "Family Retreat" during "Carnaval" time. What began as a simple event of our local church has continued and grown for thirty-five years.

I remember Tele-Esperanca (Tele-Hope, a telephone ministry)—you used answering machines to deliver taped messages for all those who called in. I remember you opening the Bible institute in our church because there were people who felt a call to prepare for the ministry. They now form a lasting legacy of many laborers sharing the gospel over the last thirty-six years.

I recall how the correspondence course Fonte de Luz (Source of Light) was launched—reaching various prisons, many parts of Brazil, and even other Portuguese-speaking countries. It is still in use today. I remember how you invested in the young people, couples ministry, puppets ministry, choir, and drama.

I appreciate all the missions' conferences. I remember your insistence that the fledgling church have a missionary vision. This has paid off. We have a missionary in China and Uruguay due to the vision you nurtured.

I remember you insisting on keeping the camp property in Jaboticabal. And so much more!

You are leaving a very important legacy. You have produced spiritual descendants. Many who are active in the harvest today—pastors, missionaries, lay workers—are faithful because you invested in their lives. This is the greatest tribute to someone who invests his entire life in the ministry: to know the work begun, will perpetuate. To God be all the glory!

May God Himself recompense you greatly.

BRAZIL

by Geneva Poole

Brazil, oh Brazil
How large you are!
Stretching north to south some five thousand miles or more
And east to west for some three thousand miles
You are a land larger than the continental U.S.
With approximately one-half of South American land area
And approximately one-half of the South American people
Whose language is Portuguese.

Brazil, oh Brazil
How beautiful you are!
A sandy coastal area
With coconut palms and fishing boats
A plateau of sugar cane and coffee fields
The mountains full of majestic beauty
And natural resources
The flowing rivers like no other country has
The Amazon to the north
And the Iguaçu to the south
With the marvelous sights to behold
Of the Iguaçu Falls and Sugar Loaf Mountain.

Brazil, oh Brazil
How steeped in darkness you are!
Dominated by Satanic forces
Manifest by large numbers of suicides, assassinations
By immorality and divorce
By robberies and dishonesty
Religious darkness
With Catholicism and her rituals on the one hand

To devil worship and spirit possession on the other
That has kept the people superstitious
With fears of hexes or curses
Fears of certain animals like black cats
Or of objects like feathers or a simple plant
Or the crossing of arms when four people shake hands
Or what might happen
If someone takes a bath right after a meal
Or eats cold ice cream and drinks hot coffee.

Brazil, oh Brazil
What a large mission field you are!
Largest of Free Will Baptist mission fields
With twenty-five states and three territories
The ultramodern areas
Taking advantage of the electronic age
Where people congregate in cities
In number up to twenty million
And also the territories of unreached, uncivilized peoples
Still living in the stone-age surroundings
Of the rain forest.

Brazil, oh Brazil
What lies ahead for you!
Since the new plan has brought uncertainties
Higher cost of living
Loss of jobs
Closing of factories and businesses
Which we trust will cause the people
To turn to God
Put their trust in Christ
And join the evangelical forces.

Brazil, oh Brazil
How desolate of the truth you are!
What spiritual needs you have!
Within the great cities where millions walk in religious darkness
Steeped in the rituals of Catholicism or Spiritism
Or within the vast areas
Where underprivileged people live
With so few schools or so little medical help
And most of all even without a gospel witness.

Brazil, oh Brazil
Cannot you hear her plea for help?

Poole's first prayer card picture (1960)

Daddy and Mama Poole
(1966)

Geneva teaching missionary children (1961)

People of the farm Village of Albertina (1962)

First day of the Sunday School in Ribeirao Preto (1962)

Second meeting hall of the first church (1964)

With my parents at the Florence, SC airport (1966)

First students in our Bible college in First Church (1973)

Ipiragna FWB Church (1977)

Marincek FWB Church (2004)

Christmas in July (2000)
(The only time our complete family has been together)

Statue of Jesus in glass casket

Voodoo dolls

*Youth of First Free Will Baptist Church
at Camp Jehovah Shammah*

25th anniversary of FWB work in Brazil (1983)

The beautiful Iguaçu Falls in Brazil

FREE WILL BAPTIST INTERNATIONAL MISSIONS

5233 Mt. View Road
P.O. Box 5002
Antioch, TN 37011-5002
615-760-6157 or toll free 877-767-7736

www.fwbgo.com

We exist to facilitate Church Planting Movements among unreached peoples.

Magazine Devotional? WOW!

Devotional Magazines for the entire Family!

Michael would love this!

That's D6!

The best way to develop a strong youth group is to invest in the spiritual development of children.

D6 Devotional Magazines for the entire family equip, motivate, and resource parents to drive faith at home. Everyone studies the same Bible theme at the same time. This gives dads, moms, and grandparents a head start on having faith talks, conversations that matter, and teachable moments that will last a lifetime.

Cool writers!

Inside these trusted resources you will find not only daily scriptural devotions, but also regular columns and articles by **Dave Ramsey, Answers in Genesis, Jim Burns, Candice Watters, Sean McDowell, Mark Matlock, Brandon Heath, Fred Stoeker, John Trent, and many others.**

Our award winning D6 Kids magazines are packed with daily devotions, articles, games, puzzles, activities, and more!

Churches can order in bulk or families can subscribe online at D6family.com.

helping parents reconnect to their kids!

Customizable for churches!
For more information call
800.877.7030

DON'T let the FEAR
of not knowing exactly what to do

hold you back
from ministering to someone.

First Aid for Emotional Hurts
Edward E. Moody, Jr. Ph.D.
ISBN: 9780892655649
$12.99

"I don't know what to say." How many times have we said those words to a friend or family member who is going through a painful or difficult time? *First Aid for Emotional Hurts* is a new book that provides the tools and knowledge needed to help others through the difficult issues in life.

Dr. Moody looks at the lives of Biblical characters such as Job, Samson, Abigail, and Tamar to give examples of dealing with issues that are prevalent today. He also explains basic medical terminology and medication that is often necessary in treatment, as well as when to seek professional help.

To order: **1-800-877-7030**
www.randallhouse.com

www.FirstAidForEmotionalHurts.com

NEW RELEASE
from Randy Sawyer

"AT LONG LAST RANDY SAWYER has pulled back the cover to expose the hidden secret of pastoral depression. Unlike other books that tend to be purely theoretical, Randy writes about his own battle with the "black dog" of depression. If you are a pastor, you will resonate with his story. If you are a lay leader, Randy will tell you how to help your own pastor. If you want to know how to win your own battle with depression, read this book. I found myself challenged by Randy's honesty and encouraged by his own journey. He's been there, he knows the struggle, and he knows how to help others. I'm glad he wrote this book because it could quite literally be a life-saver."

Dr. Ray Pritchard, President
Keep Believing Ministries
(Author of *An Anchor for the Soul, Why Did This Happen to Me?* and *The Healing Power of Forgiveness*)

"**BATTLING THE BLACK DOG** is an honest and transparent look at one of the evil one's great weapons: depression. Randy Sawyer's personal battle with this all too present foe is gripping and instructive. He has written a book that will help many. Would that more ministers of the gospel would write with such openness concerning the struggles of life and ministry we all face as we seek to follow Jesus!"

Dr. Danny Akin
President of Southeastern Theological Seminary

Visit randallhouse.com for more information

The challenges faced in ministry can easily make one susceptible to depression. Rather than ignore the problem, it is time to be prepared and win the battle. The author speaks with the voice of experience, desiring to help those in ministry find a way to overcome the profound impact of depression on the individual, the family, and the ministry.

Battling the Black Dog
ISBN: 9780892655205

Price: **$13.99 each**

Group Discounts Available!

ORDER TODAY!
Call **800.877.7030**
or visit **randallhouse.com**